T0198919

Endorsements

Joseph S. Spence Sr. wrote a gospel literary book, which is a repertoire of spiritual poems and poetic prayers about faith, praises, sacrifices, and God's love – akin to the book of Psalms – to name a few, where Christians can really acquire a spiritual connection. This book provides a new kind of narrative of the sweet language of Jesus. Great poem collection!

—*Jenny Marlon, "A Modern Day Psalm."*

"Spiritual Poetry in its truest sense!" This best describes Joseph Spence's book "Sincerely Speaking Spiritually." It's an epitome of man's overflowing feelings in simple words. His poems mirror the faces of adoration and worship to God. Spence takes the palette of simple words yet concrete thoughts, proving that some of the greatest poems come from the simplest ideas. His poems represent the voice of the faithful, ordinary people, the believers, and even sinners - A special gift not only for Christians but for humanity.

—*PJ, "Spiritual poetry in its truest sense."*

Another masterpiece from Spence, Sr! Finally, the long wait is over. It's worth the purchase. It's written by an award-winning author who writes divinely, sensible poems and prayers for Christians yearning for our Savior. He is a poet, speaker, a man of God, researcher, and book reviewer - which I admire. He is exceptional, and you really have to read his works. This is a book you can chill with daily! Not just a collection of poems, but an album of God's promises!

—*Stan Ignalaga, "Another masterpiece from Joseph S. Spence Sr."*

During coronavirus pandemic, the Word of God is needed. It comes in the form of this book by Joseph Spence. His poetic prayers bring to my mind the writings of the Bengali mystic Rabindranath Tagore. "Spiritually Speaking" requires immense concentration and would do well in a monastery for monastic contemplation. I suspect that the author practiced much meditation and prayer to compose such a magnificent work of spiritual guidance. His faith is enviable. His book requires soul searching about one's faith. We received a course in poetic forms and literary English. A worthwhile book for one's home library or opening prayers at Bible classes.

—*HBN: " Spiritual help, especially during coronavirus pandemic!"*

It's important to feed your soul what you put into it. The quality. The goodness. It's all-important. Reading this book was like a balm to my soul. My mom recently passed, and I was drained in every way. This book of poems was exactly what I needed. It's thoughtful, inspiring, and feeds goodness to my soul. These are difficult times in this world. I recommend feeding your soul, something that inspires it to kindness.

—*Sheila English, "What feeds the soul."*

Wow! This book is such a blessing. You can almost feel the worries and cares of life, leaving you, as you read these uplifting and encouraging poems. Beautiful poems, by a beautiful soul! Thank you, Mr. Spence, for sharing your talent with the world. Blessings in Jesus!

—*Reb Coleman*

This is a remarkable book of spirituality to obtain a more significant relationship with God. It's refreshing, inspiring, and uplifting to the mind, body, and soul. During this coronavirus pandemic, it brings triumph over stressful situations with a smiling face reading God's Grace in another format—"Poetry!" The words instill the love and presence of God in one's heart with much inspiration. I love the words, poems, prayers, and the spiritual Epulaeryu dishes of communion and blessings created by Joseph Spence, a man of reverence! Everyone should read this book of guidance and experience a greater awareness of God's Grace.

—*Terri Lynn Wigley, Proprietor for Terry Lynn Express.*

The Free International Poetry Exhibit and Contest

www.poetrysoup.com

August 30, 2007

Dear Joseph Spence,

Congratulations on being a PoetrySoup International Poetry contest winner. Over 1221 poems, from all over the world, were entered in the July 1, 2007 contest, so you certainly should be proud of this accomplishment. This was a very, very difficult contest to judge. Each contest, the quality of poetry gets better. That should make you accomplishment even more gratifying.

We also want to thank you for helping build the PoetrySoup community. Your poetry has significantly enhanced the PoetrySoup community. Please continue to submit your work.

Joseph, many people ask, "Why do you do this? You do not request a reading fee and you actually give out cash." Honestly, we love reading good poetry. We've said that many times before, but it really is as simple as that. As time goes on, we hope to increase the prize money.

We rely heavily on word-of-mouth "advertising", online advertising, and donations from our poets, so please tell your friends about us and continue to support PoetrySoup.

Thanks again Joseph for your poetic contributions to PoetrySoup and congratulations!

Sincerely,

Mark S. Pringle
Managing Director and President

This letter of commendation was awarded for the poem "Amazing Grace," winning first place in Poetry Soup International Contest, July 1, 2017. The poem is on page 32.

This certificate of poetic excellence was awarded for the
poem "Amazing Grace," winning first place in Poetry Soup
International Contest, July 1, 2017. The poem is on page 32.

Wisconsin Bookwatch: The Poetry Shelf

By James A. Cox, Editor-in-Chief – Midwest Book Review

Author Name: *Joseph S. Spence, Sr.* **Book Title:** *Sincerely Speaking Spiritually* **Publisher:** *WestBow Press (August 2020) c/o Thomas Nelson Publishers PO Box 141000, Nashville, TN 37214*

Synopsis: "Sincerely Speaking Spiritually" is an inspirational and uplifting body of prose poetry that is ideal for meditating on Christian principles and applying them to solve our 'real world' problems, and living a righteous life.

Additionally, The fundamental message underlying the deftly crafted poetry that comprising "Sincerely Speaking Spiritually" is that God's manifestation of preparing a table before you in the presence of your enemies is a daily reality. That every Christian can improve their standing before God and heighten the quality of their spirituality by allowing Him to anoint them with His grace, His mercy, and His love.

Critique: Occasionally graced with black-and-white images, "Sincerely Speaking Spiritually" by Joseph S. Spence Sr. begins with an informative foreword by Pastor Reverend Bradley E Coleman BA Master of Divinity. The individual poetry is as inspired and inspiring as it is meditatively compelling. Very highly recommended for all members of the Christian community, "Sincerely Speaking Spiritually" is one of those rare collections of Christian verse that will linger in the mind and memory long after the book itself has been finished and set back upon the shelf. It should be noted for personal reading lists that "Sincerely Speaking Spiritually" is also readily available in a paperback edition (9781973683919, $11.95) and in a digital book format (Kindle, $3.99).

Editorial Note: His Excellency, Dr. Ambassador, Professor, Joseph S. Spence, Sr., USA (Epulaeryu Master), is an award-winning poet and the author of over one hundred peer-reviewed published poetic articles and ten inspirational poetry books.

Source: <u>http://www.midwestbookreview.com/wbw/aug_20.htm#Poetry</u>

Sincerely Speaking Spiritually

Daily Inspirational Praise for
"Uplifting Your Soul" With God's Grace!

Joseph S. Spence Sr.

WESTBOW
P R E S S®
A DIVISION OF THOMAS NELSON
& ZONDERVAN

WestBow Press books may be ordered through booksellers or by contacting:

WestBow Press
A Division of Thomas Nelson & Zondervan
1663 Liberty Drive
Bloomington, IN 47403
www.westbowpress.com
844-714-3454

Scripture taken from the King James Version of the Bible.

ISBN: 978-1-9736-8391-9 (sc)
ISBN: 978-1-9736-8390-2 (hc)
ISBN: 978-1-9736-8392-6 (e)

Library of Congress Control Number: 2020901439

Print information available on the last page.

WestBow Press rev. date: 05/10/2024

Dedication

To my dear mother, Mrs. Olive Maud Spence (Justice), and father, Mr. Kenneth John Spence (Moses), for all the wonderful things each of you have taught me about life that I will always cherish. Additionally, to my brothers and sisters for all the wonderful times we shared and will always share together. Furthermore, to my extended family members—cousins, niece, nephews, and so on—for your inspiration. Finally, to my children and grandchildren, who will always have my love and special places in my heart. My sincerest thanks to each of you, and may God continue to shine His perpetual light upon each of you, your loved ones, and family members from generation to generation.

Additionally, this book is dedicated to the humble writers with words of ethics and integrity for worldwide literature. Those who are dedicated to uplifting heads held low to inspire them to see a new light and day. This is also dedicated to all writers who are paving a way for worldwide humanity to experience God's blessings in every way, shape, or form. And to poets who are sharing God's light to create a path of righteousness and newfound inspiration in His grace for others to walk with love and reverence in His newfound light.

Have an awesome day, don't forget to pray without ceasing, stay encouraged, be strong, inspired, ingenious, resilient, and blessed always!

Dear dedicated reader, I will be impressed with your feedback regarding how you enjoyed reading my inspirational book of spiritual poems. It inspires me to write more when readers comment, and it's my pleasure to listen to readers and be uplifted by what they say. Thank you very much for your decisiveness and dedication. Please make your comment on Amazon.com and GoodReads.com. Have a great day, and God's blessings always!

Contents

Section 2:   Poetic Prayer Forms

Section 3: Invented Short Spiritual Poetic Forms

Section 4:   Epulaeryu Poems

Section 5:   Spiritual Poetic Forms Glossary

Preface

The World's Dynamic Process—Poetry Prayer

In this inspirational book, you will learn the essence of poetic prayer and how it will uplift your mind, body, and soul.

- ✓ Inspirational poetic prayer is a dynamic and cosmic moving force for the soul. It makes a person whole and stimulates an exploration of inspiration in the spirit to its very core.
- ✓ It invokes a process of creation that inspires and connects life with God's spirit.
- ✓ It allows a person to become graciously entwined with and not maligned with life.
- ✓ It inculcates a precious quality of mind, body, and soul into reality.
- ✓ It enables an internal and external blending of one's self to obtain a medium of equilibrium even if the pendulum swings in the opposite direction.

Additionally, poetic prayers, in reality, are God's words spoken in a different form and style for greater understanding and is a unique precious language of Grace and reverence in these ways. It instills an orderly process of sanity in many ways where insanity exists. It institutes a stabilization factor bringing to reality, out of disagreement, a state of being establishing normalcy and order to a world spinning out of control. It's the more admirable quality of reality. It enhances the most precious and creative merits of life to obtain invaluable consciousness and normality.

When applied to souls avoiding redemption, they may somehow refer to poetic prayer as an elusive state of being or mind since it does not exist in a vial or test tube, where it's capable of manipulation. However, poetic prayer ascends the lack of order and bring tranquility where none existed before. It stimulates a revival of the spirit where such supposedly already exists in a state of mundane dullness. It's an ongoing and sensational revelation from God for uniting the mind, body, and soul as one entity.

Furthermore, poetic prayer enables an intertwining of the trinity in the spirit in many ways as follows:

- ✓ It's an uplifting process in which a rhapsody and essence of the soul are touched deep from within its core, causing the heart to resonate with new life.
- ✓ It stimulates new creation from God!
- ✓ It's spoken and unspoken words unto the senses yearning for a higher order of life.
- ✓ It is to be expected in a world of instability, instituting God's stability through intercession.
- ✓ It's the precious unveiling of a newly found revelation of higher existence for the mind, body, and soul.
- ✓ Poetic prayer is not static. It's action-orientated, does not procrastinate, nor lingers in oblivion.
- ✓ It's a dynamic moving force for souls to love each other, as God loves us (John 13:34). We must live in peace with our neighbors, and let not our hearts be troubled (John 14:27); thus, enhancing an uplifting of God's creation with His Grace!

Based on the above proliferation of poetry prayer and how it uplifts and enhances your relationship with our Creator, please join hands and hearts and get your copy of this eloquent spiritual text to strengthens your alliance in Grace with God's love today!

Acknowledgments

My dearest thanks to all my poetic friends for allowing me to complete this *Sincerely Speaking Spiritually* poetry book. Inspirations from each of you rendered blessings upon me during our journey. Certainly, words from each of you have been uplifting. I have definitely learned a lot over the years. The styles and forms of poetic prayer and writing we have practiced will always stick with me in my growth as a spiritual poet and writer. They have been very inspiring and educational in the process of learning how to use some of these poetic forms and styles.

My compliments and blessings to the various poetry sites on which I have been a member, participated in poetry writing and prayers, and where I have met many of you. My special thanks to Patricia Ann-Simpson, founder of *Worldwide Alliance of Poets, United Kingdom,* for having me serve as the poetry prayer chaplain for the site. Most people didn't know there was a poetry chaplain online at Worldwide Alliance of Poets. On finding out, the request for prayers opened the flood gates. Working with administrators and poets around the world on these poetry sites has been a very enlightening process for me and everyone involved with my poetry prayers.

Many thanks to my family and friends for allowing me the time to participate in helping uplift the bowed down heads of worldwide humanity. Certainly, time was taken away from you and your activities. Realizing this was a precious and godly cause, the granting of your approval without any debate or disagreement sparked enlightenment. All of you were included in the prayers and your names uplifted.

My sincerest thanks to the editors of the following journals, anthologies, and magazines in which some of my poems, book reviews, and researched articles not included in this manuscript were previously published:

Creative Launcher, Prayagraj, Uttar Pradesh, India
Cyberwit International Journal, Allahabad, India
Harvest of New Millennium, Allahabad, India
Taj Mahal Review, Allahabad, India
Parousia Magazine, Nigeria, Africa
Phoenix Magazine, Milwaukee Technical College, Milwaukee, Wisconsin, United States
Setu Bilingual Journal, Pennsylvania, United States
Sound of Poetry Review, Athens, Greece
The Edition Online, Bengali, India
Urban: Genre Creatives, Milwaukee, Wisconsin, United States
Ewriter World, Nigeria, Africa
Atunis Poetry, Brussels, Belgium

Thank you for your support and for helping me along the way. May God sincerely bless each of you always!

Foreword

Dear Reader,

I have no doubt that this collection of poetry will soothe your soul and enlighten your heart. Like a cup of cool water to one who is thirsty, my hope is that this poetry book gives you spiritual refreshment and rejuvenation.

The poetry within this book is somewhat different from other poems you may have read. Even the title, *Sincerely Speaking Spiritually,* is unique and offers a glimpse into the essence of the poems that have been gathered for your enjoyment and edification. In these poems, Mr. Spence has drawn on his vast experiences, knowledge, and travels to offer you, dear reader, a collection of unparalleled poetry filled with common sense, humor, spirituality, and wisdom.

As you read these poems—no, even before you begin to read—remove all distractions from around you. Clear your mind, and open your heart to the spiritual poetry of Mr. Spence (epulaeryu master). My prayer to the Father is that you are blessed by these poems and inspired to live your life to the fullest!

Rev. Brady E. Coleman, BA, MDiv
Pastor, Siloah Lutheran Church and School
Milwaukee, Wisconsin

Introduction

Reading this very uplifting text of God's Grace should solidify your relationship with Him. It will enlighten your soul to understand and apply the essence of poetic prayer in strengthening your love for God, and to assist others needing prayer.

Writing an inspirational poetic prayer, or a scriptural poem is not as easy an event as reciting a typical prayer. It's indeed very different from writing a regular poem. Although some of the principles are similar, a spiritual poem deals with the truth of the matter. While regular poems may be fictional in nature, the religious poem is real. This type of poem comes from one's heart and is a supplication of intercessory prayer to stand in the gap on behalf of another soul. It relates to real-life situations and is factual in words. While the regular poem uses imaginative and a variety of creative conventions, the prayer poem uses more concrete, figurative, and literal vocabulary.

The poetic forms of both may be the same in terms of narration. They use similar stanza formats, such as:

➢ Haiku, senryu, freeform, tercet, couplet, sestet, and varying octaves.

➢ Four-and five-line stanzas of quatrain, quintet, couplet, ballad, epigram, sonnet, ode, and others.

Therefore, the architecture and construction of the forms are similar. The styles and articulation of languages are mostly different in nature. However, they share corresponding themes of inspiration, motivation, and stimulus, uplifting the souls of others.

Sincerity Speaking Spiritually is divided into five sections:

> The first begins with regular spiritual poems in various narrative forms and styles.

> The second consists of prayer-poems, mostly in the freeform style.

> The third reflects a variety of invented poetry forms and styles.

> The fourth is the spiritual epulaeryu poetic form I created during my travels around the world and sampling delicious meals in fellowship with God's saints. The essence of the poetic form addresses succulent dishes and drinks. The ones in this book address spiritualty as food and drinks, uplifting the spirit.

> The fifth and last section is a glossary of the various forms and styles of poems highlighting understandable definitions.

While reading this divine text, you will also find a variety of poetry forms developed by me.

> First, as previously mentioned, is the "Epulaeryu" poetry form regarding foods and drinks from around the world. Many have enjoyed writing this poetry form on a variety of worldwide poetry online sites and in competitions

> The second form is the "Linking Pin Sonnet" regarding spirituality. It links the previous line to the next as a form of strength. I created this form based on the linking pin concept of organizational development and leadership in management. It also enhances the linking pin concept of studying the Bible for instant recall based on passages of scripture relating to real-life situations.

> The third is the "Seventh Heaven" poem. This poem requires the mentioning of seven and heaven in the lines in a spiritual

context, making it flows with reverence and Grace for the reader as its identifying principle.

➢ Finally, "God's Dynamic Steps," in which the title, the upward steps, and poetic lines are illustrated in fives (5 x 5 x 5).

Based on the preceding, obtaining your copy of this publication, reading, and sharing its revelation with friends and loved ones will rejuvenate and uplift your mind, body, and soul for a more excellent relationship with God and His abiding Grace.

Get your copy today! Have an awesome day, don't forget to pray without ceasing, stay encouraged, be strong, inspired, ingenious, resilient, mindful, enlightened in God's Grace, and blessings always!

Section 1
Regular Spiritual Poetic Forms

꩜ ～＊— ⌇

My People, if We Must Die

My people, if we must die,
let it not result from being unable to serve the cause for the betterment
of humankind or from being denied a seat around the table in the land
of the free and the home of the brave.

My people, if we must die,
let it not result from anger and reprisal against each other instead
of sitting down in peace and love to bring about God's blessings,
understanding tranquility, and a true quality of life.

My people, if we must die,
let it not result from the thirst or want of righteousness and lack of
God's salvation, like dry bones with no voice rotting away in a valley
of condemnation without God's grace.

My people, if we must die,
let it not result from the lack of beautiful songs stimulating our souls,
with God's love radiating from the magnificent choral voices of our
children and grandchildren immersing themselves in our great cultural
heritage of wisdom, knowledge, spirituality, and understanding.

My people, if we must die,
let it not result from the agony of an unscrupulous person lacking God's
grace and wisdom, ripping off our safety deposit boxes and cleaning
out our bank accounts while we are tucked away in an old folks' home
somewhere.

Alas, my brothers and sisters, if we must die,
let it be after, and only after, our souls have passed on the renaissance
knowledge of God's grace, blessings, and mercy to all humankind,

like a shining star created by God, gliding across the universe from the
East to West, one that raises aspiring heads and beaming eyes,

opening up wondering minds and joy-filled hearts molded by God's
hand, leaving on the tongue of all who seek to reach for it,

words of everlasting hope— "I wish!"

Then, and only then, if we must die, only God in heaven awaits us!

> "My People, if We Must Die" is dedicated to the
> memory of Claude McKay, Harlem Renaissance poet
> from Jamaica, West Indies.

Your Time Has Come

Your time has come like the rising sun. Stand up for life created by God's love like a dove descending from the vaults of heaven with an olive branch. He has a plan for you to be one with Him as He is with you, thus making you brand new. Your life should be more than just an ordinary existence. Allow Him to strengthen you as your soul runs the distance. Be filled with His spirit, and let His light shine in you real bright. Manifest His joyful glory. Overcome obstacles in His name while unto Him, you render acclaim. Move ahead, and be the lighthouse of strength without relent, thus ascending from the bottomless pit into His eternal light of creation. Experience the fullness of your faith with God in the middle of your future. Build your foundation on His words and spirit. Empower your soul with His tenacity; He will determine your capacity. Be anointed by His grace, and experience the reality of not just a dream but also a light lit for living liturgy. He has you covered with His Holy Spirit. Now step out: Your time has come!

His Perpetual Light

Looked God's people down,
Knocked His saints down.
Ran His loving people down,
Tried to burn His followers down.
Shoot at them around the globe,
Left them for down while running around.
Tried in ways to tear them down;
From the dust they rise by the potter.
Always standing in His light,
Triumphantly staying alive.
His love always in their sight.
Believers helped them to stand.
Based on His resurrection plan,
With His power and might.
Like Saul relieved of his sight,
He is waiting to bring you
Into His perpetual light!

> Dedicated to those who have felt the pain of being
> thrust aside and marginalized for no apparent reason.
> Marginalization of others is not a splendid way of life,
> especially for those who have felt the agony of being
> cast out onto the sidewalk or trashed.

Joseph S. Spence Sr.

We Are Still Standing

Through it all, never,
Never should God's people fall.
Fall never; through it all,
God's people are still standing!

Anchored in His foundation,
Standing on a solid landing,
Trusting always in His grace.
Leaning on His broad shoulders,
Believing in His holy words.
Words that shall not be moved,
Moved only by His promise of love.
Love upholding His people in faith;
Through it all, never fall.
God's people are still standing!

Your Omnipresent Love

I will declare and decree You have made me in Your own image.
    You created me.
Hearken upon the voice of my cry, my heavenly King.
    You hear me.
Mine eyes are consumed because of grief, yet Your love dried them.
    You comforted me.

I consider the heavens the works of Your fingers, the moon and stars.
    You ordained me.
Who shall abide in Your tabernacle and dwell in Thy holy hills?
    You exalted me.
You kept me as the apple of Thine eyes, under the shadow of Your
wings.
    You protected me.

In You, I placed my trust when others tried to persecute my soul.
    You liberated me.
When the sorrows of hell compassed me about with snares of death,
    You encompassed me.
When I rest my head to sleep and am awakened from my slumber,
    You sustain me.

"I put your whole armor on me to stand against the wiles of the devil," *
    You protected me.
I placed my trust in You from everlasting to everlasting.
    You preserved me.
From the daunting enemy, those who hated me, and those too strong
for me,
    You delivered me.

According to my righteousness and cleanliness of my hands,
  You recompensed me.
They left me in calamity; You brought me forth to a larger place.
  You uplifted me.
"A bow of steel is broken by my arms, and I am girde with strength." *
  You armored me.

Your shield of salvation I carry, and Your right hand holdeth me up.
  You made me great.
I will give thanks unto You, and sing praises to Your name forever.
  You are my great redeemer and deliverer!

  *Ephesians 6:11.
  *Psalm 18:34 and 39.

In Times Like These

In times like these,
Just call Him, and you will be pleased.
He will put your mind at ease.
Call Him now, please!

He awaits your plea.
Lay your cares at His feet.
With Him, your troubles will be relieved;
He will fill you with glee.

He is there and will give you an answer;
There is no need to ponder.
He will bring you back like the crack of thunder,
Putting your mind at ease with His wonders.

In times like these,
Believe in His everlasting power.
He will rain down His loving shower.
Call Him now; don't be a fence dancer.
In times like these, He has the answer!

> This poem consisting of quatrain and quintet stanzas
> is dedicated to those seeking the right answer. In times
> like these, we need a Savior. Many are weary and don't
> know where to turn. There is a choice, and that choice
> is God, our Creator. Be very sure your anchor holds
> and firm grips His solid rock!

Joseph S. Spence Sr.

Love Is

Love is patience and waiting on her while exhibiting God's grace.
Love is not displaying arrogance when she is defenseless.
Love is giving her a kiss when she burned out the engine in the car.
Love is never giving up on her; when times are hard, never part!
Love is endurance in keeping her alive with a God-blessed smile.
Love is seeing her in God's image when you're upset.
Love is not winning at all cost with your chest and lips poked out at her.
Love is rubbing her back and feet at night when they hurt.
Love is scratching her back when she can't reach it.
Love is making her breakfast in bed with a smile when she is tired.
Love is giving her your last piece of pancake with syrup at breakfast.
Love is God's image smiling in your heart with grace for her.
Love is the smiling face of God you see in her eyes at all times.
Love is God's will in you for her with His unconditional love!

Anaphora poem: The first word in each line beings with the same letters throughout the poem.

Christ Lives Today

Christ, our Savior,

Lives today.
His mighty power
Is shown each and every day.
His unending love is here to stay.
He lives today in many ways.

Christ, our Redeemer's,

Awesome healing miracles
Live not only in spectacular circle.
He removes illnesses and pain,
Allowing His saints to make greater gains,
Giving life He sustains.

Christ, our shining star,

Beautiful name of mercy,
Lives in all our hearts.
He creates all of its working parts.
As the potter molds us from the clay,
He creates us in His own way.

Christ, our King on high,

His name reigns in the land.
God is the person with the master plan.
He is always there to give a hand
When we fall and cannot stand.
He is waiting to wrap us in His angelic band.

Christ lives today!

> This poem consisting of sestet stanzas is dedicated
> to the body of believers. Christ is the name through
> which we shall be saved. Believe in Him, place your
> cares at His feet, and follow His guidance.

Your Time Has Come—Welcome!

Believe it, achieve it, now conceive it.
Look at it, go for it, and behold it.
Heads up, eyes to the sky—God's glory.
Shoulders back, no slack—it's His story!

Eyes open, you've been chosen—His citizens.
Reach for Him, go for it—He is risen.
Motivation high—He is always glorified.
Aspiration to the sky—He is magnified!

Inspiration never dies—His love applies.
Barriers down for us; He has the crown.
Ceilings crash—His light now in sight.
Mountains moved, it's our time to unite!

Ain't going back—no time to sidetrack.
Heading for the top—no time to stop.
Rise up from the dust, receive His kingdom.
Your time has come—He says, "Welcome!"

Joseph S. Spence Sr.

If Only: Parent's Challenge

There are times when I contemplate
Why children come to school late.
Sometimes I even try to relate
Why parents from the rules deviate.

If only children and parents would get along,
Things would be great in the land.
If only children would show respect,
Then things would probably be perfect.

The Good Book has some special words
Regarding children that must be heard.
It also has God's special directions
For parents seeking heaven's elevation.

If only parents and children would listen,
They would shine and just glisten.
If only they would work as one,
They would be on track with God's plan.

But on earth many say there is no utopia;
To the other side they must cross over.
If only they would hold God's unchanging hands,
Then together, they would make a mighty stand!

> This quatrain stanza poem is dedicated to parents and
> children working together in unity on God's plan.

His Ecclesiastical Love

As the sun's photosynthetic rays touch the ecosystem and natural things,
As the moon's magnificent glow brightens a quiet lake and gives lovers wings,
As a gliding star skips across the galaxy with the wish of a silver bell's ring,
His ecclesiastical love touches our hearts and makes creation sing!

The Love of God

The love of God brought us from clay to this day.
By His love, He is the potter, molding us in many ways.

The love of God has opened our eyes to see.
Like He touches the blind man at the pool, He has touched me.

The love of God has called His Son to bear our cross.
Climbing the hill to Calvary His love has paid the cost.

The love of God has opened many doors we agree.
As He opened the tomb and walked, He sets us free.

The love of God has paved a way for us to walk.
His shining star protects our feet from evildoers' talk.

The love of God has protected us from perilous wrath.
By His mercy and grace, He still shows us His path.

The love of God has sated our hunger.
By His grace, He provides us manna like thunder.

The love of God comforted us and made us free.
By His love, He always hears and responds to our plea.

The love of God is strength to our souls.
His knowledge leads us and makes us whole.

The love of God is always in our hearts.
His shield and buckler quench the flaming darts.

The love of God grants my plea.
God's guardian angels are protecting me.

The love of God dwells always in our hearts.
Our love dwells in Him, and we shall never part!

This couplet poem is a response to a challenge from
another poet to write a poem regarding the love of
God. It is written in the rhyming couplet format. May
we give Him all honor and glory!

His Returning Presence

He came down to earth upon His birth
To deliver humankind and improve their worth.
He walked the land and healed the sick,
Elevating even those limping with a stick.
He spoke the words, and it was done,
Cleansing hearts of many as the day begun.
His loving touch was all it took,
Healing many as written in the Golden Book.
With love for us He was slain.
He went away for us only to return again!

> This poem is dedicated to His returning presence.
> The Christmas season brings His presence into our
> midst. With praise and thanksgiving, we celebrate His
> name with beautiful songs. This is a glorious season
> around the world. It is the time of the year when
> humankind focuses their hearts, minds, bodies, and
> souls on the shining star with loving care of His birth.
> Prepare for His returning presence!

Merry Christmas Greetings to You

To each of you, I send this special cheer.
Wishing you Merry Christmas with loving care.
Your warmth has forever touched my heart.
I knew it would from the very start.
Merry Christmas greetings to each of you.
Stay beautiful in whatever you do.
Though some days may be bleak and dark,
Your ship will come for you to embark.
We belong to a family with special love.
May God's blessings descend on you from above.
I pray that your future will be fruitful and bright
As you continue to walk in His eternal light!

Have a Merry Christmas.
Happy Hanukkah.
Happy Kwanzaa.
Happy holidays.
God bless!

This poem is dedicated to all of God's people. Please
make this Christmas a special one with friends and
family. Also, remember those who are less fortunate
because we are all precious in His sight. Look forward
to the future with great enlightenment, and keep
expecting that great expectation. Merry Christmas,
Hanukkah, Kwanzaa, and Holiday to each of you.
May God touch you and your loved ones with His
blessings!

Christmas Beauty in You

Christmas love for our family.
Keeping us in blessed harmony.
Christmas peace of mind,
Allowing us to be ever so kind.
Christmas quality of life,
Taking us above human strife.
The beautiful Christmas season from God,
Instills in us His Son's love we have.
May His peace always see us through.
His Christmas beauty shines in you.

This poem is dedicated to families and friends at Christmas. Being with family and friends during the Christmas season is truly a blessing. This poem focuses on the essence of relationship and love for each other in relation to how God gave His Son to us. The radiating essence of Christmas brings joy to our hearts, peace to our minds, and inspiration to our overall beings as we celebrate His birth and love in a special way.

Praising Him All the Way

I am praising God today,
Glorifying Him in a mighty way.
My faith in Him will not sway.
His love for us is here to stay.
Praising Him all the way.

My faith in God is a solid anchor.
I shall not be moved even by a clanking tanker.
Believing, trusting, loving, and praising.
Wearing His armor day to day.
Praising Him in a mighty way.

God is my solid foundation.
On His rock I shall forever stand.
Shining His light throughout the land,
My faith in Him is mighty strong.
Praising Him all the way!

> This quintet poem is dedicated to the saints who are praising and those who want to praise His name. Rendering praise and thanksgiving to God is uplifting. We see clearer, feel better, and come to know Him greater. Keep praising Him every day, in every way, all of your days!

Sunday Thoughts

To the Sabbath for many.

Sacraments of love now on my mind.
Universal atonement for all humankind.
New Jerusalem to be revealed in time.
Disciples praising Him, standing in line.
Acolytes are leading and reading today.
Yuletide greetings are not too far away.

Troubles lifted in daily prayer.
Honoring our dear Savior.
Our souls He cleanses and protects.
Under His wings we are perfect.
Gaining His wisdom and love.
His praises daily we lift up above.
Thanks for today and our journeys of life.
Salvation is ours from His stripes!

> This acrostic poem is dedicated to worshippers on
> the Sabbath day. They pray for others in intercession
> to heal their pain and improve their lives. Their
> relationship with God is very sincere.

Mothers

*M*others are truly God's gift to the world and really for us.
*O*h, they will put things out, even a fuss, with a simple touch.
*T*he essence of their being prevents us from being in a rush.
*H*ear their words of wisdom, and one will learn very much.
*E*ven as drivers they shift gears without scraping the clutch.
*R*esting a child's head, they simmer a cry with such a hush.
*S*aving grace, loving us dearly, like a hand with a royal flush!

This septet acrostic poem is dedicated to all mothers
on their special day. Mothers are specially sent from
God into this world to heal its pain. They are the
backbones and field marshals of the family. Their
maternal instincts are very awesome.

His Loving Easter Touch

He gave His life for me and you.
His precious love for us is always true.
He came to earth to heal the strife.
For me and you He gave His life.

Healing many, He walked the earth.
Blessing mothers giving humanity's birth.
Touching those without a penny.
He walked the earth, healing many.

With loaves and fish, He fed many.
After dining, they had plenty.
They ate even without a silver dish.
He fed many, with loaves and fish.

To save humankind, He gave His life.
Laid down His soul for all our plights.
His love and grace for us combined.
He gave His life to save humankind.

The world has been touched by His love.
Easter comes to us like a dove.
Season of grace, He gave us much.
By His love, the world has been touched!

Today's Victory

Victory today shall be mine.
While climbing this rugged incline,
He strengthens me to run this race,
Moving closer to heaven's place.

Victory utters from my tongue.
Saints of glory I am among.
At this place I cannot go wrong.
By His grace, I am always strong.

Victory overwhelms the soul.
His mercy's light never grows old.
Wrapped in the garment of His love,
His light shines on me from above!

Love of the Father: New Heights

Our Christian heritage thinking.
    Setting the stage for living.
        Healing the lame and the sick.
            Feeding those who are hungry.
                Clothing those who are naked.

Our love for His Son, Jesus.
    Uplifting the souls of humankind.
        Restoring sight to the blind.
            Strengthening our love and faith.
                Establishing a solid foundation.

Our belief in God the Creator.
    Thanking Him for His creation.
        Praising Him for His consecration.
            Confirming peace in our hearts.
                Elevating lives of God never part!

Without the Love of Jesus

The tomb would be sealed.
            Redemption unheard of.
                        Saving grace unknown.
                                    Darkness on the earth.
                        Crucifixions still rampant.
            Amazing grace not possible.
Life would be with no value.
                        Without the love of Jesus,
                                    Barbarians rule!

His Great Manifestation

My day is determined
    By His Word in me.
        Rejoicing in His name,
            Not by the world around me.
                Every day He has made,
            His Word lives in my heart,
        Bringing great manifestation,
    Love, life, and living Lord.
Such illuminating magnification!

He's Coming Back Again

He's coming back again.
Some are wondering when.
Will it be know or then?
The good news is,
He's coming back again.

He is the great I Am,
Coming back for everyone.
He has a salvation plan.
The good news is,
He's coming back again.

Singing glory alleluia.
He is the almighty Savior.
Promise Him your best behavior.
The good news is,
He's coming back again!

Joseph S. Spence Sr.

Creating Artistic Words Linking Pin Sonnet

We are natural poetic creators,
Creators of the artistic words.
Words that uplift the soul,
Souls pouring out, reaching out.

Out to the world for redemption,
Redemption of the inner spirit.
Spirit of natural sanctification,
Sanctification stimulating the mind.

Mind of elevating jubilation,
Jubilation of living creation.
Creation pointing the way,
The way to the supreme Creator.

Creating natural poetic words,
Words uplifting His blessed birth!

The next poem is also a linking pin sonnet.

Crying Out Sonnet

There is a suffering world crying out.
Crying out for a great revelation.
Revelation of the Holy Spirit.
Holy Spirit of sanctification.
Sanctification of grace with God's love.
God's love rising up mighty people.
People endowed with His most sacred trust.
Sacred trust outpouring over the earth.
Earth divinely created by God's hands.
God's hands molding people in His image.
Image crying out for God's divine love.
Divine love of God, the gracious Father.

There is a suffering world crying out.
Crying out for God's great revelation!

Amazing Grace

"Amazing Grace," a well-known spiritual song, was authored by John Newton, a former slave trader. It's probably the most beloved hymn of the last two centuries. John Newton, who wrote the hymn, was born in 1725 in London. While serving on a slave ship during the voyage home, it was caught in a devastating storm and almost sank. Newton prayed to God to spare his life and he would give up slave trading in return. The cargo miraculously shifted to fill a hole in the ship's hull and the vessel drifted to safety. Newton took this as a sign from God and his conversion to Christ. Newton later convinced member of parliament, William Wilberforce, to seek the abolition of slavery. In 1764, Newton, was ordained as an Anglican priest and wrote 280 hymns. He wrote "Amazing Grace" in 1772. It was published in "Olney Hymns" in 1779. Under the leadership of William Wilberforce, the English government outlawed slavery in 1807 and Newton lived to see it. The passage of the Slave Trade Act is depicted in the 2006 film, "Amazing Grace." One of the first Historical Black University and College, Wilberforce University, was established in 1856, and named after, William Wilberforce, the abolitionist in England who engineered ending the slave trade with inspiration from John Newton. The university was constructed as a joint venture between the Methodist Episcopal Church and the African Methodist Episcopal Church.

Sources
Sheward, David. "The Real Story Behind 'Amazing Grace.'" *Biography.* 3. https://www.biography.com/news/amazing-grace-story-john-newton. O'Conner, Allison. "Wilberforce University (1856-)." *Black Past.* https://www.blackpast.org/african-american-history/wilberforce-university -1856/.

Amazing Grace

The soul whom God's Son sets free
    with His graceful love is free indeed.
Unlocking the rusting shackles
    of unjust and disgusting oppression.
Allowing life's amazing grace
    to shine with His loving embrace.
Transformation of soul's deep darkness
    to light's stimulating brightness.
Uplifting the revelation of God's truth
    As Jehovah revealed unto Ruth.
His extraordinary and infinite power
    shining His abiding love every hour.
Preservation and living hope for life,
    His love abounds with no strife.
How sweet the wonderful sound;
    No other around to be found.
Wrapped in His everlasting embrace,
    Sweetly singing, "Amazing Grace"!

Significant Comment: Amazing Grace won The Poetry Soup International Poetry Award of Excellence International Poetry Contest, July 1, 2007. It received the "Recognition of Outstanding Poetic Achievement Poetry Soup Award." The award certificate was signed by Mark Steven Pringle, Managing Director and President.

Kind God Who Made Us Glad-Monotetra

Omnipresent merciful God,
Cleanse all hearts today that are bad.
Too many people are so sad.
They will be glad! They will be glad!

Look upon Your people with grace.
Let them know life is not to waste.
Draw them to stick to You like paste.
Erase disgrace! Erase disgrace!

Your words have uplifted many heads
With a prayer as they go to bed.
Show them Your gracious light instead.
For them You bled! For them You bled!

Gracious Father of humankind,
In us let Your Holy Spirit unwind.
Your grace shall leave no one behind.
You are so kind! You are so kind!

Praising Him Always

Praise Him above with all glory.
He spread His love, touching hearts below.
His love is such a great story,
One giving hearts a fiery glow.
He leads me in the path of His love.
Let me fly like one of His loving doves.

He spread His love, touching hearts below.
One giving hearts a fiery glow!

He has sheltered me with His wings.
His angels lift my feet on high.
He has taught me such precious things.
His glory has opened mine eyes.
I will forever sing His praise.
World desires will never erase.

His angels lift my feet on high.
His glory has opened mine eyes!

Comes what may on this precious day,
My Savior will open the door.
His great light has brightened my way,
Yet I seek His face for much more.
His love and glory are precious.
With them I will always be illustrious.

My Savior will open the door,
Yet I seek his face for much more!

God's Autumn Season

An

Uplifting revelation of transformation in the natural process of earth,
Touching its beauty with autumn season when hues of golden leaves inspire souls.
Undivided attention to the essence of God's love bringing new life and glory,
Majestically earth sings and tells a new story.
Newness of life for humankind to behold His wonderful glory!

An

Omnipresent God, omnipotent love, omniscient being.
Season of love and thanksgiving for all to experience His great joy.
Stimulating celestial sights of splendor and light from His kingdom.
Elevating thoughts for everyone in His magnificent grace.
Now and forever, the essence of His love we will embrace!

Most Gracious God

He loves us; He cares for us.
His love so great,
Heals hearts and unites them.
Makes our hearts glow like fire.
Such gracious,
Everlasting,
Heaven's love.

Like the sun's sparkling rays
From above,
His love glows within us.
Like a bright shining light
On the path,
Leading the way
To heaven's stairs.

We raise our heads to the sky.
And we climb
Steps on Jacob's ladder.
In the right direction,
His light leads.
Hearts following
Gracious God.

Thank You, Lord, for This Great Treat

This turkey must be pulling my leg.
If not, it must be Thanksgiving.
Give me some cranberry sauce.

This looks oh, so very nice.
It also smells graciously charming.
Place a side of dressing on my plate.

Let me bless this Thanksgiving bird.
Thank You, Lord, for this great treat.
Now I need some tasty pumpkin pie.

The kind with the crispy edges.
So soft and delicious inside.
Pour me a glass of sweet iced tea.

The kind that goes well with my meal.
Now, before I sit in paradise.
Let me bless this Thanksgiving bird.
Thank You, Lord, for this great treat!

The Master's Favor

Like a fountain, it pours on my head.
My filled cup now running over.
Receiving blessings from on high,
The Master's way of showing favor.

Taking care of my daily tasks,
Extending a hand to my fellow man.
Blessings I receive from my Maker.
Like a fountain, it pours on my head.

Showing love is not hard to do,
Extending it straight from the heart.
Blessings I receive from my Maker.
My filled cup now running over.

Touching hands with people each day,
Loving the way each heart smiles.
Like showers from above it pours,
Receiving blessings from on high.

We should do what we can afford.
Blessings will be received in return.
Helping others to help themselves,
The Master's way of showing favor!

God never breaks His promises.

The Narrow Path

Narrow,
Nearer,
Guides like a dove.
Always
Cheerful,
Charm from above.

Graceful,
Grateful,
Guiding the way.
Peaceful,
Giving,
God's love will stay.

Living,
Laughing,
Majestic days.
Caring,
Sharing,
Singing His praise!

Joseph S. Spence Sr.

Father of Light

After the storm, there will be a calm,
Like a revival of the soul.
Where darkness was once on a face,
Now calmness erupts in grace.

In the beginning there was void
Darkness on earth, one could not avoid,
Not even the squeak of a light.
Mankind was to be blessed unknown,
Although no obedience shown.
Hands of knowledge moved in darkness.
With its touch, no sign of weakness.
It was the beginning of time.
The Creator had things in mind.

Light He commanded, which converged.
Darkness erupted and exhorted
As the earth's mass He converted.
Father of light for all ages asserted!

Precious Savior

His precious love for us is here today to stay.
The potter molds us from clay His own way.
He is the One with the master plan.
There are times we fall and cannot stand.
He always gives a helping hand
With His angelic band.
He is the King
With Whom we win.
The great Master,
No disaster.

He gives a helping hand
With His angelic band!

He allows His saints on high to make greater gains,
Removing tears, stress, illness, and signs of pain.
He performs great healing miracles.
He lives in specific circles.
Heavenly redeemer,
Christ, the precious Savior.
He lives today.
Lives in our hearts.
Brightens our day.
He is here to stay.

Heavenly redeemer,
Christ, precious Savior!

Joseph S. Spence Sr.

Sun Shining Love

Beautiful sunlight shining bright,
  Snow slowly melting, bringing forth new light.
    Warming the soul with such a soft touch.
  Couldn't ask for much.
Now blush!

The crack of dawn melting the morning dew,
  If one only knew such heavenly hue.
    Wrapped in golden light,
  Such an inspiring delight.
Treasured love without any spite.

Wonderfully sweet heavenly bliss,
  Such love one never missed
    God's warm hugs.
  Natural love from above,
Eyes fluttering like soft wings of a dove.

Heaven knows what's right.
  He is always all right.
    Moment's pleasure one can treasure.
  Love surrounding without any measure.
Elevating the soul in its natural light!

Heaven's Freedom

Christ, we love You most of all,
Your wondrous work, grace, and love.
Your power has made us stand tall.
Your mercy is like the sent dove.

Your kindness stirs one's soul and life.
Your greatness gives life every day.
You remove from our hearts all strife.
You sustain our hearts in Your way.

Christ, You have showed us the light.
Please maintain with us now Your peace.
You also taught us how to live right,
You apply Your love and not cease.

Please, Father, touch us with Your hand,
And bless us with Your precious touch.
As always, You shine in the land.
Your precious saving grave is our plan.

Christ, we love Your sweet grace.
Now Master, please hear this, our plea.
In heaven we shall see Your face.
Gracious Savior, with You we are free!

Joseph S. Spence Sr.

God's Glory

The heaven declares such beauty.
The love of the Father shines forth.
Take His hands as is your duty.
Testify unto Him your worth.

Heavenly Father, help us now.
Hear our solemn plea and our cry.
Have Your angels look at us with eyes of a sparrow.
Heal our hearts pure as You know how.

Elevate us as Your servants.
Expect the best from us to You.
Everlasting, Thou are constant.
Evermore and forever true.

Lift us up with Your glory.
Look over us, Your humble sheep.
Leave on our tongues Your great story.
Love us now, even when we sleep!

God's Desire

Wonderful light of day.
Goodness of hope for all
From the Creator's way.
At the cross we stand tall.
Such love with us must stay.
Your grace prevents us from a fall.

Your mercy endureth forever and ever.
Your lovely spirit adorns and leaves us never.
Your sweet smile radiates our souls and endeavors.

Your love for us endureth.
Your wondrous work is marvelous.
You're the One from Nazareth,
Always shines, never ambiguous.
All things You knoweth and seeth.
You create us advantageous.

We seek Your face, know You; bless us.
Your love for us is contagious.
We call on You, singing great hymns.
You want us to be ambitious.
You want us all, fat or slim.
Your love for us is courageous!

Joseph S. Spence Sr.

Escaped in a Basket: Paul Bringing God's Light

They went left. He went right.
Lost them? *Not so fast,* they thought.
He went up, they went down.
Soldiers with arms he without.
Like cat and mouse.
Command voices overshadowed their steps.
Was he now trapped in a corner?
It was scary at best.
Neighbors hushed. He did not have a house!
They wanted him!
He could not even see a way out.
They were confused, could not catch him.
Captured? He refused!
Things looked so grim.
Then out a window with a basket.
A thin shadow never submits.
Neighbors in love, he was lowered.
Just like a dove, so inspired.
His name—Apostle Paul.
Escaped into the night.
Stood mighty tall.
Bringing God's light!

Looking Out Today—The Window of Live (Visualization Poem)!

As I looked out today, I see,
> People moving diligently, with the purpose of God ordering their steps.
> Some smiling, rushing, walking, crawling, but all pressing onward.
>> As state in Philippians 3:14 "I press toward the mark for the prize of the high calling of God in Christ Jesus."

As I looked out today, I see,
> Blue sky, birds flying, chirping, sipping nectar from flowers.
>> Trains moving, planes flying, rain from clouds, a rainbow forming.
>> As stated in Revelation 4:3 "And he that sat was to look upon like a jasper and a sardine stone: and there was a rainbow round about the throne, in sight like unto an emerald."

Looking out today, I see,
> Concrete highways, cars busily driving, bikes riding, skate boards zooming.
>> Life moving along, happily, not sadly, showing God's inspired grace.
>> As stated in Ephesians 2:8 "For by grace are ye saved through faith; and not of yourselves: it is the gift of God."

Looking out today, I see,
> Mended fences, beautiful gardens growing, God's inspired children smiling.
>> Sad people not crying, seeking a new way, a new day and new light.
>> As stated in Corinthians 4:16 "For which cause we faint not; but through our outward man perish, yet the inward man is renewed day by day."

As I looked today, I can see,

Opportunities for growth, roses blooming, nice fragrance smelling.
New possibilities of life beaming, darkness shattering by God's light.

As stated in Ephesians 5:8 "For ye were sometimes darkness, but now are ye light in the Lord: walk as children of light."

As I look out today, I see,

A new horizon generating from the evening red sunset.
Uplifting a nation in unity, with God's love, prosperity, and blessings.

Enhancing one's quality of life, to reach high—like a shining, star!

As stated in Revelation 22:16 "I Jesus have sent mine angel to testify unto you these things in the churches. I am the root and the offspring of David, and the bright and morning star."

Section 2
Poetic Prayer Forms

This section has prayers for individuals with various ailments. If you're aware of someone who is suffering from an ailment that matches the prayer—such as a friend, loved one, colleague, or family member—personalize the prayer for those you know who are in need. Blessings always!

Prayer for Readers

Blessings to you, my dearly beloved brothers and sisters. The Word of God states, "He knows our heart even before we come to Him in prayer. He also knows what's on our tongue before they are spoken" (Psalm 139:1–4). Therefore, we must be penitent when we approach Him in grace and prayer. Having faith in our prayers, we shall receive what we asked for (Mark 11:24). Today, I pray with faith and a heart deserving of what God wants. May His love, grace, and blessings be with each of you always in your life's journeys as you read these prayers and make an intercession for others. May He lift each of you always to know His ways and stay in His grace by following His prescribed path. May He protect each of you from the fiery darts of the enemy by clothing you in His whole armor of salvation (Ephesians 6:10–18). May He give you victory over all adversity, like He gave to King Jehoshaphat, who prayed bowing down upon the earth when his enemies marched against him in war (2 Chronicles 20). May He lengthen the life of each of you upon the earth as he did for Hezekiah, who prayed with his face turned to the wall (2 Kings 20:1–6). Also, may your days be always blessed and free from illness in His name from generation to generation.

Prayer and Poetry Historical Notes

Prayer and poetry alter the consciousness and give a deeper perception of life in reaching out to others. Poetry and prayer unfold mysteries and bring about a deeper sense of reality. Poetry existed before literacy in *The Odyssey* (800–675 BC). The combination calms the mind and brings relief in the form of intercessory prayer when one stands in the gap for others, which was an Old Testament priestly function, and currently the pattern of Christ in the New Testament. The biblical basis for the New Testament believer's ministry of intercessory prayer is the calling to be as a priest unto God. His Word declares that we are a holy priesthood (1 Peter 2:5), a royal priesthood (1 Peter 2:9), and made us kings and priests unto God and his father (Revelation 1:6). Therefore, we pray for others and for their healing. It's on this basis of bonding our intimate relationship with God that we can stand "between" Him and others, serving as advocates and intercessors on their behalf. One example of a prayer poem is The Wessobrunn Prayer Poem also called by some "The "Wessobrunn Creation Poem." The poem is named after the monastery at Wessobrunn, Bavaria. This has been the repository of the sole manuscript, which is now the Bavarian State Library, Munich. The date of composition is around c790, while the surviving manuscript dates from about 814. The place of origin of the manuscript is unknown. The poem is in two sections: the first is a praise of creation in nine lines of alliterative verse, and the second is the actual prayer in free prose. The two together constitute a prayer for wisdom and strength to avoid sin. The poem has been recorded in music many times in the 20th century. The most recent interpretations by composers in the classical tradition include Felix Werder in 1975, for voice and small orchestra, and by Michael Radulescu in two works: *De Poëta* in 1988 for four choirs and bells, and another arrangement in 1991, re-worked in 1998 for soprano and organ.

Source

"The Wessobrunn Prayer." *SansaAgent.com*n.d. http://dictionary. sensagent.com/wessobrunner%20gebet/en-en/.

Prayer for Our Soldiers

Dear heavenly Father,
Please bless our soldiers wherever they may be.
You know the trials they have to bear.
You know the threats they are facing.
You know their expectations.
You know their hearts.
You know their pain.
Protect them!

Heavenly Father,
Please bless the families of our soldiers.
Reduce their anxiety.
Provide them with strength.
Give them Your victory.
Grant them patience.
Put Your loving arms around them.
This is their time of great need.

Also, heavenly Father,
Guide and strengthen them.
This prayer is for our men and women in uniform.
Intercede on their behalf.
Lift their burdens.
Shine Your light upon them.
Continue to show them Your love.
Grant them Your peace.
Amen!

❧

Prayer for Father's Day

Dear merciful and gracious God,

The Supreme Father of wisdom, knowledge, and understanding.
The guiding light of all creation.
Leader, provider, and Good Shepherd of our fathers.

I call on you today in a mighty way in intercession for our fathers.
Guide their feet while they run this race.
Strengthen their hearts as they walk Your way.
Cleanse their thoughts as they strive to stay on Your path.
Provide them with hope as they pray with Your love each day.

Touch their total being as a family foundation.
Show them wisdom as they counsel their children and young generation.
Open their hearts to family values and the gospel.
Walk with them, and guide their feet around sinking sand.
Listen to their pleas all around Your land.

Mold them as You are the potter, and they are the clay.
Teach them how to kneel with their children and pray.
Talk with them as they would with their children and family.
Impart divine wisdom, knowledge, and understanding upon them.
Wrap them in Your mercy, and surround them with Your glory.

These blessings I ask as Your humble servant.
In the name of Your only begotten Son, Jesus,
The morning star of all creation.
Singing praises unto His name
Henceforth until everlasting.
Bless each father today and always.

Amen!

This poem is dedicated to fathers who are walking the walk and talking the talk in honor of their children. I thank God for my father. He was the kind of person who, when the dinner table was set, you didn't want to be late. His stories were entertaining and victorious, his instructions always helping and meritorious, and his praises to God uplifting and glorious. May he continue to rest peacefully in God's kingdom!

Prayer for All Children

Dear God,
I call upon You today,
Asking You to bless all children in Your mighty way.
Grant them protection while they play.
Keep them safe from danger and out of harm's way.
Intercessory prayer, I plead for them as I pray.

Heavenly Father,
Grant them wisdom.
Teach them how to use their common sense.
Protect them from worldly nonsense.
Keep them from those who inflict harm through pretense.
Guide them in using all their senses.
Gracious Savior,
Go with them swimming for safety.
Let them not make decisions drastically.
Place upon them your armor protectively.
Teach them to obey their parents reverently.
Let them not squander their resources haphazardly.
Blessed Redeemer,
Guide them with Your mighty hands.
Children are hurting all over this land.
Reveal unto them Your salvation plan.
I know You will do everything that You can.
Teach them how to righteously stand.

Dear gracious One,
You are the same yesterday, today, and tomorrow.
Keep their steps away from places of horror.
From their faces remove all sorrow.
Give unto those in hospitals needing bone marrow.
Look over them with the eyes of the sparrow.
Amen!

As You said Jesus, "Suffer little children, and forbid them not, to come unto me: for of such is the kingdom of heaven" (Matthew 19:14). This poem is dedicated to all children around the globe and across the spectrum for their safety, growth, and protection. Children are hurting today and are in pain. This prayer is for children anywhere and everywhere. Some are so innocent and without blemish. May God heal their hearts and provide them with love and protection.

Joseph S. Spence Sr.

Prayer Against Suicidal Thoughts Inflicting Souls!

Most gracious and merciful Father,
Creator of heaven and earth,
Knower of all things seen and unseen.[1]
Forgive everyone contemplating suicidal sin.
Open the doors for all to avoid such thoughts.
There is always room at the cross.
St. Augustine, 5th century, condemned suicide as a sin.[2]
Thomas Aquinas, 13th century, denounced suicide,
As an act against You, who know our hearts.[3]
Put demonic suicidal beliefs on the run.
The price has been paid by Your precious Son.

Most precious and heavenly Father,
Wash suicidal beliefs away with Your holy water.
Take everyone with doubt to the alter.
Lift up those with suicidal thoughts lingering.
Cleanse their hearts of this contrary sin.
Bring all unbelievers to know You.
If they only knew what suicide will do.
Show them Your almighty power.
Erase their fears and suicidal words every hour.

---

[1] Psalm139:8, shows God's omnipresence.

[2] St. Augustine, 5th Century, in his book "The City of God," delivered the first condemnation against suicide as a violation of the 6th and 9th Commandments. Source: Ortiz, Dr. Jared. "Saint Augustine Contra Suicide." *The Catholic World Report.* 2019. https://www.catholicworldreport.com/2019/09/29/saint-augustine-contra-suicide/.

[3] Thomas Aquinas, 13th Century, denounced suicide as an act against God and a sin, with civil and criminal laws enacted, resulting in the confiscation of property. Source: Battin, Margaret, ed. "The Ethics of Suicide Digital Archives: Thomas Aquinas (c. 1225-1274)." *Oxford University Press.* 2015. https://ethicsofsuicide.lib.utah.edu/selections/thomas-aquinas/.

Show them the way of Your salvation.
Save them from suicidal grave damnation.[4]
Touch those fostering suicidal will from frustration.
Focus their minds, bodies, and souls on You.
Erase every suicidal pressure making the souls brand new.
Grant them forgiveness from suicidal stressfulness.
Make them believers and teach them what's right.
Show them Your everlasting and uplifting light.
Teach them how to pray and lead them Your way.
Your acceptance shines mercy with everlasting glory.
Gracious Father hear our prayer against suicide.
In the name of Jesus, we pray,
Heal every heart from suicidal thoughts.[5]

Amen!

---

[4] Catholic Catechism 2281: Suicide contradicts life and is a gravely contrary to the just love of self, and 2325: Suicide is contrary to justice, hope, and charity and forbidden by the Commandments. Source: Paul, Bishop, John, ed. "Catechism of The Catholic Church 2nd Edition." *Vatican Council*. 1997. http://www.scborromeo.org/ccc/p3s2c2a5.htm#2281/

[5] Jews against suicide: Some Jews consider suicide as a sin. The probation of suicide is mentioned in the Talmud. Some Jews believe it's a result of death by a disease or disorder and there is no outright prohibition. Suicides allowed in some instances are now questioned and believed the lives of those committing suicide would have been spared. Source: Gordon-Bennett, Chaviva. "Judaism's View on Suicide." *Learns Religion*. 2019. https://www.learnreligions.com/judaisms-view-on-suicide-2076683.

Prayer for Thanksgiving Day

Dear merciful and gracious God,
Supreme Father of all blessings,
The One who provides food, clothing, and shelter.
The guiding light of all creation,
Leader, provider, and Good Shepherd of us all.

I call upon You today in a mighty way.
Please shed Your love of Thanksgiving on Your people.
Bless them with a delicious meal for Thanksgiving.
Strengthen their hearts as they walk Your way.
Give them strength and love to provide for their family.
Provide them with hope as they pray.
Sustain them with Your love from day to day.

Touch their total being and family foundation.
Show them wisdom to provide wise counsel.
Open their hearts to impart Thanksgiving and the gospel.
Walk with them and guide their feet around sinking sand.
Listen to their prayer all across Your land.

Mold them as You are the potter, and they are the clay.
Teach them how to strengthen the family and pray,
Especially this upcoming Thanksgiving Day.
Impart divine wisdom, knowledge, and understanding upon them.
Wrap them in Your mercy, and surround them with Your glory.

These blessings I ask as Your humble servant.
In the name of Your begotten Son, Jesus,
The morning star of all creation.
Singing praises to His holy name,
Henceforth until everlasting,
Especially on Thanksgiving.
Bless us all today and always.

Amen!

Prayer to Cease Gun Violence in Schools

Dear God,
I call upon you today,
Asking you to bless all children in Your way.
Grant them protection while they study and play.
Keep them safe from danger and out of harm's way.
Dear Lord, I plead for them as I pray.

Holy Redeemer,
Guide all teachers with Your mighty hands.
Teachers and children are hurting all over this land.
Reveal unto them Your salvation plan.
Teach them how to righteously stand.

Heavenly Father,
Bless all parents of students.
Guide and comfort them in taking care of children.
Touch and comfort parents who have lost children.
Look over the schools they attend and guard them.
Protect them from shooters and school violence.

Dear God,
You are the same yesterday, today, and always.
Protect children, teachers, and parents from horror.
From their faces remove all pain and sorrow.
Bless those in all school systems from all danger.
Look over them with the eyes of the sparrow.

Dear God,
Look at the individuals carrying guns.
Let them know it's no fun to shoot others.
Show them that Your way is one of peace,
That school violence should immediately cease.
And this type of tragedy shall not repeat.

This is our humble plea:
To eliminate school shootings.
We pray and send unto thee.

Amen!

There have been many school shootings across America and the world. Please, everyone personalize this prayer for any particular school, college, university, or circumstance. Children in schools need added protection from violence by troubled people. Blessings!

Section 3
Invented Short Spiritual Poetic Forms

The definitions for the following forms are located in the "Glossary." It explains the way each form was created, the creator, and date of creation.

Mother

A
Mother
So divine.
Children she loves.
Angels brightly smile on her from above!

Quadruple Senryu

God's Might

God my guiding light
sustains me in all my plights
hold me with Your might

God's Love

His love is so true
filling me all through and through
moves from me to you

God Forever

His grace lasts always
makes me say God I will not
forget how to pray

Have Faith

bitterness shall not
have victory over souls
a new dawn will come

> This quadruple senryu poetic tercet series is dedicated to individuals seeking a new path and new light of life. The form was created in Japan. It does not use punctuation, and capitalization is limited to proper nouns.

Joseph S. Spence Sr.

New Peaceful Dawn

mornings in summer
birds sing melody of grace
pleasing harmony

walking in His light
peace and joy come with His love
creation of dawn

> This haiku duo tercet, created in Japan, seventeenth
> century, is dedicated to who walk in His morning
> light with the rising sun. Daily morning walks are
> great to clear the mind and relax the body and soul.
> Peacefully walks in His morning light allows one to
> enjoy His splendor and beauty. With a gentle breeze
> against the face, such a walk also focuses a person to
> become one with His majestic creation in experiencing
> a new peaceful dawn with God's created nature.

Reaching God through Steps

Trusting Him always./
Tell God you'll stay./
From His loving ways./
Stay His course; don't stray./
Praise God every day./

For His Love I Search

Coming from above/
His abiding love./
Hold His graceful love./
Find His precious love./
Search now for His love./

This quintet duo series of "God's Dynamic Steps" focuses on God's love and praising Him. They were created by Joseph S. Spence Sr., (me) on March 10, 2007, while studying English literature, creative writing, and poetry at University of Wisconsin-Milwaukee. There are five steps to ascend, and five syllables on each step with a rhyming sequence. The title has five words matching the steps.

Joseph S. Spence Sr.

Sadness

(Negative Emotions: We Don't Practice)

Seclusive negative spirit of a kind.
Acquiescing darkness of the mind.
Denouncing the bright smiles of life.
Needling others to react with spite.
Exposing one's self to simple gloom.
Spreading the language of doom.
Selfishly drowning the joy of creation.

(Turning Negative to Positive Emotion)

Self-satisfaction with life's journey.
Assurance of friendship with love.
Deliverance from the pit of despair.
Nectar of life's happiness flowing.
Exemplified with such cheerfulness.
Spirit of jubilation all encompassing.
Serenading the love of life's beauty!

> This acrostic septet duo is dedicated to those who are
> willing to turn sadness to gladness. Sadness comes
> with the turf sometimes. However, the objective is to
> overcome such a negative state of mind and implant
> one of joy and hope internally for others to see
> externally and be inspired by your reflection of joy.

Covenant Made

The mandate was laid.
A covenant with God made
To share and persuade.
His love came down upon us.
Blessing others in His trust!

This quintet tanka poetic form created in Japanese seventh-century, is dedicated to those who are uplifting the mandate. Binding God's spirit in our souls is a covenant that should never grow old. It keeps us focus on entering the pearly gates!

God's Reflecting Light

God's Glory

glory beams on high
by His grace praises rendered
His love on their tongues

God's Light

light from the kingdom
stream from heavenly Father
rainbow after storm

His Light
a ray of light shines
God's blessing for all to see
illumination

This trilogy tercet senryu series may be written in different styles. It may deviate from the strict traditional Japanese senryu form. Punctuation is not used in the senryu poem. Capitalization applies only to all proper names. However, this senryu style is in the 5/7/5 syllable format, normally consisting of three lines and seventeen syllables. It addresses an emotional state of being or may be satiric, unlike the haiku that addresses nature.

God's Eternal Enlightening Strength

Peaceful Growth

Growing in His grace,
Enlightenment guides the path.
Blessings of love now flowing.
Majesty of life.
Elevation for the soul.
Doors open for peaceful growth.

Clearing the Path

The path is narrow
Leading to eternal light,
Where burdens are laid in faith.
Many have been called.
However, few are chosen.
Standing in His light with strength!

Jubilation Day Celebration

The day of jubilee is coming.
The day when God will deliver.
The day when His grace will favor.
The day when you will be delivered.
The day is in your sight and grasp.
The day waits for you to reach for it.
The day of your jubilation!

> The anaphora septet poem starts with the same words
> in the beginning of each line. This one relates to God's
> coming jubilation.

God's Reflecting Angelic Seven Septet Series

His Words

through His mighty words
power manifestation
when you obey Him

His Faith

faith is evidence
inner substance of the soul
God fulfilling needs

Open Doors

God will open doors
always shut by humankind
He will make a way

Revelation

the day is coming
truth shall be revealed on earth
evil shall not win

His Angels

the spirit of God
angels standing by His saints
love insulation

Repentance

trusting in His words
repentance of mortal souls
it is time to pray

His Baptism

God will bless His saints
as they walk through the fire
with His baptism

Joseph's His Servant—Testament!

Joseph, the dreamer, His servant,
    Enslaved by those in the dark.
        Female bearing false witness.
        God always delivered him.
    He displayed a heart of pure gold.
True testament of God's love!

> One does not have to look too far in today's society
> to find a modern-day Joseph. Just blink, and you will
> see one being thrown under the bus. This sestet poem
> highlights the story of Joseph, God's noble servant
> and dreamer.

God's Rejoicing Success

Rejoicing Spirit

Rejoicing in life.
       Soul's jubilation singing.
            Raising of voices.
      Praises of joy unto Him.
Uplifting mortal spirit!

Overcome It

The fear of failing.
       Worrying about success.
            Remove it and live.
      Walk through the opening doors.
See yourself overcoming!

> This tanka quintet duo series focus on the spiritual
> power within to see it through and overcome. Release
> your thoughts, and elevate yourself above obstacles.
> Move over the mountain or around it; you don't have
> to crash through it. Think about it, save your breath,
> breathe deep, and see your way to a higher level. This
> tanka poem, created in Japanese seventh-century,
> touches on the essence of the human spirit.

God's Faithful Love Series

Keep Life Alive

Accept the option.
Direction of truth and life.
Immerse in God's love.
Preserving His creation.
Keep life alive in His name!

The Calling

Heed to the calling.
Serve in ways never dreamt of.
God's love is moving.
He instills the faith in us.
Help others see His bright light!

> Tanka poem is a fifth-century Japanese quintet poetic form. It has a total of thirty-one syllables written in five lines of five, seven, five, seven, seven syllables. One may say that the senryu and the haiku, which were derived at a later date, are shorter versions of the tanka poem.

Joseph S. Spence Sr.

Relative Compound Inheritance Strengthening Duo

God's Inheritance

We are God's inheritors,
Set to inherit
His gift of inheritance!

My Strength

The great Lord is strengthening.
My soul He strengthens.
Daily He provides me strength!

Relative Compound tercet poem was created by Alvin Othto Stewart. It's a three-line poem in the terset form. The subject word must be at the end of each line. The syllable count is seven, five, seven.

Relative Compound Savior's Elevation

Savior's Love

He is a loving Savior.
His love is saving.
The pure love of Jesus saves!

His Elevation

Wait for God's elevation.
He will elevate.
His love is elevating!

God's Eternal Victory Duo

His Precious Love

His precious love from above
Touches many souls like an eternal spring.
Flows gently like seven doves.
Sitting, standing, bringing praises we all sing.
He holds us like hand in glove.
Joy from heaven to lives of many He brings.
Praise Him all the way—great King!

Pressing On

Pressing on to victory.
Surrounding angels protect my daily step,
Guiding the path with their light.
Lift me above the miry clay from slipping.
Heavenly host by my side.
All seven days I will give thanks unto Him,
Praising His heavenly name!

> Seventh Heaven septet poem form was created by Joseph S. Spence Sr. (me) on October 21, 2006. The odd lines have seven syllables (lines 1, 3, 5, 7), and the even ones eleven (lines 2, 4, 6). Rhyming is optional; however, it's a plus. Any variation of the words "seven" or "heaven" must appear in the poem.

God's Radiating Light

Heads Up

Keep your head up high always.
Always look up to heaven in time and space.
His love looks down upon you,
On all seven days, radiates all around,
Touching His great creation.
Uplifting brand-new beings with His love and grace.
Sanctified with His spirit!

Shining Light

Rose of Sharon, shining light,
Your angel's beauty seven days keeps us bright.
Streaming from heaven with love,
Blessings come to us like raindrops from above.
Starry light twinkles at night.
Wish on a shining star—You heal our plight.
Fill our hearts, make us right!

Joseph S. Spence Sr.

Blessings Naani Trio

Covering

Comes from above like raindrops.
Covering the heads of those
Who are so gracious
To receive His blessings!

Grace

His loving grace
Smiles upon us always,
Keeping our hearts open
To receive His pure light!

Love

On Calvary's hill,
Shining gentle as a candle,
Flickering in the evening wind,
His shining love!

The Savior Lives

Jesus the Savior lives today.
His love so sweet and is complete.
Touching the world in His own way.
Jesus the Savior lives today.
The potter He molds us from clay.
And not to be sifted like wheat.
Jesus the Savior lives today.
His love so sweet and is complete!

Pray, Pray, Pray

Pray for peace on the earth.
Every hour, filled with power.
Pray to God; He gives birth.

Pray for God's light to shine.
Radiate seen and the unseen.
Cleansing hearts also thine.

Pray goodness for humankind.
Love thy neighbor as they labor.
Uplift body and mind.

Pray for prosperity
And saving souls, making them whole
With all sincerity!

Glorifying on High

Greetings from above, we hail.
Great blessings from the constellations.
Gathering all the forces we sail.
Glittering with universal vibrations.

Glorifying the heavens above.
Glossing with silver glow we shine.
Glowing like an angel with love.
Glorifying with the heavens we combine.

Grey battlefields down below.
Grazing green fields up on high.
Grievance out the door we throw.
Goodbye to the bad guy!

Joseph S. Spence Sr.

Thy Loving Mercy Prayer

Dear Lord,

Please send Your angels to watch over me.
Your humble servant seeks only Thee.
I am normally weak, but Thou art strong.
Strengthen my soul, and remove all that's wrong.
O Lord, my God, I need You every hour.
No one can beat Thy wondrous power.
Heavenly Father, hear my humble cry.
Sometimes I sit and try to wonder why.
Thy loving mercy is everlasting.
Dear God, be with me in sleep and waking.

Amen!

God Is

God walks with me
For everyone to see
I am never alone.

He takes my hand.
With Him I firmly stand.
Like a dove I have flown.

He died for all.
Like the cross, we stand tall.
In Him many have grown.

God is alive.
Calvary revives.
His love is full blown!

The Coming King

Voices on high look to the sky.
Harkened unto the call and see
Angels with wings doing great things.
Singing is where I ought to be.

Voices ringing, angels singing.
Listen to the splendorous sounds.
Raising of heads, even in beds.
Blessings and mercies abound.

Praise Him with strings and many things.
His majesty is to behold.
The coming King, even with wings.
His love is so great yet untold!

The Master

When faced with a challenge, brace against the storm.
Hold your head up, look to the sky, and then smile.
Remember, God's victory will make you warm.

Hold unto His unchanging hands for a while.
He will not let go; He has a plan for you.
The storm will pass, and everything will be worthwhile.

Pray for God's love, and all your prayers will come through.
He will show you how much you are versatile.
He is the King and will give you a breakthrough.

Pray to Him, the Creator of all our lives.
He is the Master who's on time when He arrives!

Joseph S. Spence Sr.

Redemptive Light

Sunlight brightens the day for all.
Nightlife fades away to lightness.
Light of hope shines with such brightness.
Spark from light's ray makes darkness small.

Awakened, man now standing tall,
With dew dripping in politeness.
Sunlight brightens the day for all.
Nightlife fades away to brightness.

God's man of vision named Paul,
Arose and filled with faithfulness.
God showed him favorableness
As he answered the mighty call.
Sunlight brightens the day for all.

Forgiveness Tears

He
Shed tears
For the loss
Of those who have
Chosen life's wrong path.
The tears He shed
Will touch them,
Return
Them.

Smile.
Some turned
Around new.
Others did not.
The tears He once shed
Are still cleansing
Soul's darkness
Into
Light!

Joseph S. Spence Sr.

The Light

God is shining bright,
Cling to His great light.
He loves everyone.
Come and take a stand.
A part of His plan.

God loves the world.
The people, too.
He creates all
In His own way.

Sunlight day,
Stars at night.
God always.

Precious.
So kind.

God!

Walk Beside Me, Lord

Help
Me, Lord,
To walk in
Your humble ways.
Know Your noble truth.
Grow always in Your love.
Seek Your path of righteousness.
Live by Your abiding knowledge.
Believe in You always as my Lord.
Keep Your faith each day as I walk with You!

The Cross: King Jesus (Tanka Quintet Duo)

Mary's Womb

One day on the cross.
Crowned with thorns around His head.
Laid Him in a tomb.
Thought He had died from His wounds.
Now love fruit of Mary's womb!

A Mighty King

He died on the cross,
Cleansing us of sins and strife.
Gave up our loss.
The almighty King named Christ
Gave for all, His earthly life!

His Resurrecting Light Tanka Quintet

Placed in a walled tomb,
He did not die from their wounds.
Dark days passed, no word.
Resurrection on the third.
Now they lift their hands in praise.

Section 4
Epulaeryu Poems

This section consists of epulaeryu spiritual septet poems. The form and style were created by Joseph S. Spence Sr. (me) on December 20, 2006. The form of the poem is 7/5/7/5/5/3/1. The form and style were developed based on my worldwide travels while serving with the US Army and cover succulent dishes and drinks. The spiritual epulaeryu is a special style of the form. It regards spirituality and biblical text.

This spiritual epulaeryu is based on John 6:1–14, when Jesus fed a multitude of five thousand.

Feeding Miracle

Meal from barley loaves and fish.
A boy with a wish.
Everyone had a fish dish.
Five thousand plus ate.
Words from the Savior.
Souls filled with
Food!

This spiritual epulaeryu uplifts the essence of Leviticus 19:10. It addresses God speaking to the owners of vineyards, and telling them, "Thou shalt not glean thy vineyard, neither shalt thou gather every grape of thy vineyard; thou shalt leave them for the poor and stranger." Also, Deuteronomy 23:24, where God told the people, "When you come into your neighbor's vineyard, you may eat your fill of grapes at your pleasure, but you shall not put any in your containers."

My Vineyard

Let the poor in my vineyard
Gleaning and eating.
Even strangers must attest.
Come to the harvest.
Sweet grapes for the souls.
Behold thy
Feast!

This spiritual epulaeryu is based on Genesis 25:34: "Jacob gave Esau bread and pottage of lentils; and he did eat and drink, and rose up, and went his way: thus, Esau despised his birthright."

Lentil Soup and Bread

Pottage of lentil and bread.
Thank You, Lord, now fed
With wheat, barley, and flour.
Filled cups this hour
Overflow with grace.
Bless this taste.
Yes!

Significant Comment: Lentil Soup and Bread won the semi-finalist position of placing 273 out of a total of 1034 worldwide poetry entries in Poetry Soup International Poetry Contest, March 6, 2008.

This spiritual epulaeryu is based on Matthew 26:2 (Pesach feast), Exodus 16:35 (manna until Canaan), Mark 6:41 (bread and fish), John 2:3 (turned water in wine), Proverbs 8:17 (God's love), and Romans 5:15 (God's grace).

Breaking Bread

The feast of the Passover,
Manna from heaven,
Seven loaves and a few fish,
Brothers breaking bread.
Wine at the wedding.
Precious love.
Grace!

Joseph S. Spence Sr.

This spiritual epulaeryu is based on John 6:51 (Bread of Life), Exodus 16:35 (manna to eat), John 4:14 (springing well), Proverbs 11:30 (lost souls), 1 Corinthians 10:16 (saints' communion), John 6:48 (Bread of Life), and Matthew 1:16 (Christ).

Saints' Communion

Feed us with your Bread of Life,
Like heaven's manna.
Your springing well quenches thirst,
Reviving lost souls.
Saints' communion.
Bread of Life—
Christ!

This spiritual epulaeryu is based on 1 Corinthians 10:31. When one is eating or drinking it should be performed in the glory of God. Also, Matthew 26:26, regarding Jesus blessing bread and saying, "Take eat this is my body."

Church Dinner

Fried chicken and warm corn bread.
Greasy fingertips.
Fellowshipping church members,
Eating and talking.
With sweet iced tea, they
Royally
Dined!

This final spiritual epulaeryu is based on John 2:1–10, where Jesus changes water into wine.

The Best Taste

He told them to fill the jars.
After they taste it.
Took a cup to their master.
Why saved this for last?
At Cana's wedding.
This is great
Wine!

Concluding Prayer

Thank you for reading my noble and inspiring book, *Sincerely Speaking Spiritually*. May God continually bless you today in all your endeavors. May He touch your entire body from head to toe with His grace and mercy. May He connect every limb, joint, vein, artery, bone, muscle, cell, part, and fiber—including your thoughts, words, and deeds—to work in His favor. May He remove every pain, negative feeling, symptom of illness, adverse invading thought, and the like from your mind, body, and soul. May He lead you in the path of His righteousness, clothe you with His armor, and radiate His aura around you. May His appreciation and commendation touch your soul and keep you whole. God didn't add another day to your life because you need it. He completed the job because someone out there needs you.

As He states in 1 Timothy 2:1, "I exhort therefore, that, first of all, supplications, prayers, intercessions, and giving thanks, be made for all men." May He wash you over again with His love, grace, and mercy. I don't believe He brought you this far to leave you.

May God continue to shed His perpetual light upon you, your loved ones, family members, and endeavors from generation to generation.

May these words of my mouth and meditations of all our hearts be acceptable in Your sight now and forever, dear God, our strength and Redeemer.

Blessings always.
Amen!

Section 5
Spiritual Poetic Forms Glossary

This defines the forms and styles of poems read on the previous pages. Some of the definitions are in depth. Some specify dates of creation, names of the inventors, and revisions into another form or style.

Acrostic poem: Formed by writing a word, which may be the poem's topic, vertically down the page. Use only one letter for each line. Each line should pertain to the word or title. Some may recommend using a phrase without rhyme; however, one may use a complete thought with a rhyming sequence. Source: Turco, Lewis. "Lyric Poetry." In *The Book of Forms: A Handbook for Poetics, 3rd Edition*, Page 121. New Hampshire: University Press of New England 2000.

Beacon of Hope poem: Starts with a sestet followed by a triplet. Then followed by twelve lines with eight syllables each. The subject is spiritual. The rhyme scheme is optional. Centering the poem, it appears like a lighthouse beacon of hope. Source: Jussaume, Christina R. "Spiritual Encouragement, Vol. 1, Comfort with Words." *www.apfpublisher.com.* 2010.

Charisma poem: Created by Christina R. Jussaume on September 23, 2010. The subject must be spiritual or about nature. Each stanza has ten lines. The syllables for each stanza are twelve, eleven, nine, eight, six, six, four, four, four, and four. The six-syllable lines must rhyme and become a refrain after the stanza. Source: Jussaume, Christina R. "Charisma Poem." *Worldwide Alliance of Poets* n.d. http://pfppublishers.com.

Cinquain poem: Consists of five lines that do not rhyme. Created by Adelaide Crapsey. Source: Good, Tree. "Section Two: Poetry Forms with Examples." In *The Language of Poetry Forms*, 45. Maryland: Publish America 2007.

Count Up poem: A titled form consisting of ten lines. The first line has one syllable, and each succeeding line adds a syllable for a total count of fifty-five-syllables. This form allows both rhyme and meter. There is only one stanza in this poetry form. Source: "Passion for Poetry: Count Up." *Worldwide Alliance of Poets*n.d. http://pfppublishers.com.

Dramatic poem: A form of poetry with drama, tragedy, comedy, monologue, dialogue, or soliloquy. Source: Turco, Lewis. "Chapter III: Traditional Verse Forms." In *The Book of Forms: A Handbook of Poetics, Vol. 3.,* 109. New England: University Press of New England 2000.

Diminished Hexaverse poem: A poem of stanzas with five lines, then four lines, then three lines, then two lines, and ending with one word. The syllables in each stanza correspond to the number of lines; that is, five in each line in the first stanza, four in the second stanza, and so on. Source: Carney, Tatyana. "Diminished Hexaverse Definition." *PoetrySoup.* 2005. https://www.poetrysoup.com/dictionary/diminished_hexaverse.

Epulaeryu poem: A poem about succulent dishes and drink, the form was developed by Joseph S. Spence Sr. (me) on December 20, 2006. The name was selected after touring the Mediterranean, Far East, America, and other places, enjoying succulent and nourishing meals. It consists of seven lines with thirty-three syllables. The first line has seven syllables, the second five, the third seven, the fourth five, the fifth five, the sixth three, and the seventh one syllable, which ends with an exclamation mark, expressing delight about the meal. Each line has one thought about the meal. Source: Spence Sr., Joseph S. "Section Five: Interlude Succulent Epulaeryu Poetry." In *The Awakened One Poetics, Vol. 2.,* 116–26. Allahabad, India: Rochak Publishing 2010.

God's Dynamic Steps poem: Invented by Joseph S. Spence Sr. (me) on October 3, 2007. The poem represents elevating thoughts going up a set of stairs or a ladder to reach higher levels of God's inspiration. The title has five letters. The poem has five steps to get to the top, and the lines are dynamic in thoughts of no more than five syllables (5 x 5 x 5). The form symbolizes an achievement, accomplishment, or the like in growth of the mind, body, and soul with God.

George's Dragon poem: Created by George, January 23, 2012. It consists of twenty lines and four stanzas with syllables as follows: stanza 1, eight, ten, nine, five, two; stanza 2, ten, nine, five, two, eight; stanza 3, nine, five, two, eight, ten; and stanza 4, five, two, eight, ten, nine. One may use any subject. Rhyming pattern is optional. Source. George. "Passion for Poetry: George's Dragon Poem." *Worldwide Alliance of Poets*n.d. http://p.f.p.publisers@gmail.com.

Haiku poem: A Japanese poetry form, the Haiku Society of America notes that the haiku may be written in different styles, which may deviate from the strict traditional form. Most haiku poems are written in the 5/7/5 format with seventeen syllables, and addresses nature. Contemporary haiku poems may be written with less than seventeen syllables. Source: Cobb, Kathy L. "Haiku and Senryu." *Shadow Poetry.* 2001. http://www.shadowpoetry.com/resources/haiku/haiku.html.

Jesus Tears poem: Created by Dorian Petersen Potter consisting of nine lines. The subject must be spiritual or uplifting in nature. One may use as many stanzas as desired, but there must be at least two. Line 1 has one syllable. Line 2 has two syllables. Line 3 has three syllables. Line 4 has four syllables. Line 5 has five syllables. Line 6 has four syllables. Line 7 has three syllables. Line 8 has two syllables, and line 9 has one syllable. Source: Potter, Dorian P. "Jesus Tears Poem." *Worldwide Alliance of Poets*n.d. http://pfppublishers.com.

Kyrielle Sonnet poem: There are fourteen lines, three rhyming quatrain and a nonrhyming couplet. The Kyrielle sonnet has a repeating line or phrase as a refrain in the last line of each stanza. Each line within the Kyrielle sonnet has eight syllables. The French use the first and last lines of the first quatrain as the ending couplet. This reinforces the refrain within the poem. The rhyming scheme for a Kyrielle sonnet is usually either AabB, ccbB, ddbB, AB or, AbaB, cbcB, dbdB, AB. Source: Chase, James D. "Kyrielle Sonnet Poem." *Shadow Poetry.* 2003. http:// shadowpoetry.com/resources/wip/kyriellesonnet.html.

Linking Pin Sonnet poem: This sonnet was developed by Joseph S. Spence Sr. (me) on January 15, 2007. It consists of fourteen lines, each with eight to eleven syllables. The end of each line links with the next. The concept is based on the principles of leadership in accomplishing a task in an organization. Strengthening organizational echelons at each level comes by connecting each element with a linking pin of leadership, thus obtaining maximum productivity in the completion of its goal. One should visualize each linking pin connecting to the next to ensure strength and safety in moving every adjoining part to reach maximum potential in mission accomplishment. Additionally, the linking pin sonnet resonates as two lovers on the same sheet of music linking together, singing the same song, and moving in the same direction while strengthening each other and overcoming obstacles, strengthening their goals, and bringing success and victory as one. This is like the practice of jumping the broom at African American weddings as a couple. Source: Spence, Sr., Joseph S. "Linking Pin Sonnet." *Atunis Galaxy Poetry.* 2019. https://atunispoetry.com.

Metamorphic Transition poem: Created by Dena Farrari, it may be written on any subject. Source: Farrari, Dena. "Metamorphic Transition Poem." *Worldwide Alliance of Poets*n.d. http://pfppublishers.com.

Mystic Wind poem: Created by John Henson on February 21, 2012. It has five stanzas of four lines, each line having eight syllables. The second word of each line must be a two-syllable word. All other words must contain only one syllable. The rhyme scheme is abab, cdcd, efef, ghgh, and ijij. It may be written on any subject. Source: Henson,

John. "Mystic Wind Poem." *Worldwide Alliance of Poets.* 2012. http://pfppublishers.com.

Octave poem: A poetry stanza with eight lines. Source: Turco, Lewis. "Chapter III: Traditional Verse Forms." In *The Book of Forms: A Handbook of Poetics, Vol. 3.,* 220. New England: University Press of New England 2000.

Pantoum poem: A poem with repeating lines throughout as a refrain. Source: Padgett, Ron, ed. "Pantoum." In The Teachers & Writers Handbook of Poetic Forms, 125. New York: T & W Books 2000.

Prose poem: Written in prose form and style, this poem does not have line breaks or other varying formatting as in many regular poems. During the mid-nineteenth century, Charles Baudelaire published *Petis poemes en prose.* Oscar Wilde, T. S. Eliot, and others have written in this style. Though started in France, it is now used worldwide. The use of concrete language and figurative speech—such as imagery, rhymes, personification, contrast, simile, metaphor, alliteration, and abstraction—may be used based on the desire of the poet. The piece may focus on language, a story, or something similar, all based on the choice of the poet. It's written in normal prose as an essay or composition, using regular sentences. Source: "Prose Poem." *Poets. org*n.d. https://poets.org/glossary/prose-poem.

Quatrain by Letters poem: Created by Erich J. Goller on July 29, 2011, it involves taking any letter from the alphabet and beginning each line with that letter. It may be written on any subject. The quatrains are unmetered; the rhyming pattern is abab, cdcd, efcf, ghgh, and so on. Source: Goller, Erich J. "Quatrain by Letters Poem." *Worldwide Alliance of Poets.* 2011. http://pfppublishers.com.

Quatrain poem: Consists of four lines of verse with a specific rhyming scheme: aaaa, abab, abba (envelope rhyme), aaba (Omar Khayyam's favorite style), and aabb. Source: Good, Tree. "61: Quatrain: My

Lullaby." In *The Language of Poetry Forms, Volume 1*, 102. Maryland: Publish America 2007.

Quintet poem: A form of five lines in each stanza. Source: Turco, Lewis. "Traditional Verse Forms." In *The Book of Forms: A Handbook of Poetics, Vol. 3.*, 228. New England: University Press of New England 2000.

Redondilla poem: A Spanish form of poetry, it has four lines with eight syllables in each line. The rhyme scheme varies from aabb, abab, to abba. It may be written on any subject. Source: Turco, Lewis. "Traditional Verse Form: The Redondilla Poem." In *The Book of Forms: A Handbook of Poetics*, 230. New Hampshire: University Press of New England 2000.

Rondel poem: A French poetic form, it consists of thirteen lines, two quatrains and a quintet. The rhyming pattern is ABba abAB abbaA. The capital letters are the refrains or repeats in each stanza. Source: Brewer, Robert L. "Rondel Poetry Form." *Writer's Digest.* 12. https://www.writersdigest.com/whats-new/rondel-poetry-form.

Sedoka poem: An unrhymed poem made up of two three-line poems called a katauta, each with a five, seven, seven syllable count. A sedoka, pair of katauta as a single poem, may address the same subject. Source: Turco, Lewis. "Lyrical Poetry: Sedoka." In *The Book of Forms: A Handbook of Poetics, Vol. 3.*, 249. New Hampshire: University Press of New England 2000.

Senryu poem: A Japanese form and style, the Haiku Society of America notes that the senryu may be written in a variety of styles. Such styles may deviate from the strict traditional form. Most senryu poems are written in the 5/7/5 syllable format with seventeen syllables, and addresses emotion. Contemporary senryu poems may be written with less than seventeen syllables. Source: Cobb, Kathy L. "Haiku and Senryu." *Shadow Poetry.* 2001. http://www.shadowpoetry.com/resources/haiku/haiku.html.

Septolet poem: A form with two sets of seven lines with a total of fourteen words. It has two stanzas with a break between them. Source:" In *The Language of Poetry Forms, Volume 1,* 17. Maryland: Publish America 2007.

Septet poem: A form with a group or set of seven lines. Source: Turco, Lewis. "Chapter III: Traditional Verse Forms." In *The Book of Forms: A Handbook of Poetics, Vol. 3.,* 249. New England: University Press of New England 2000.

Sestet poem: A form with six lines. Source: Good, Tree. "Section One: The Jargon of Poetry 43: Sestet." In The Language of Poetry Forms, 17. Maryland: PublishAmerica 2007.

Seventh Heaven poem: A seven-line form created by Joseph S. Spence Sr. (me) on October 21, 2006. The odd lines have seven syllables (lines 1, 3, 5, 7), and the even ones eleven (lines 2, 4, 6). Rhyming is optional; however, it's a plus. Any variation of the words "seven" or "heaven" must appear in the poem. Source: Spence, Sr., Joseph S. "Seventh Heaven Poems." *Atunis Galaxy Poetry,* 2019. https://atunispoetry. com/2019/08/10/joseph-s-spence-sr-usa.

Stepping Stones poem: Created by Ralph Stott, it consists of any number of verses. It has six lines of two, two, four, two, two, four syllables. The first two lines start with the same letter, and the last two lines start with same letter. Line 3 and line 6 must rhyme. This make a nice story poem or gradations from light to dark, silence to sound, and the like. Source: Scott, Ralph. "Stepping Stones Poem." *Worldwide Alliance of Poets* n.d. http://pfppublishers.com.

Swap Quatrain poem: Each stanza contains four lines. The first line in each stanza is reversed with the fourth line. Within each stanza, line 1 must rhyme with line 2. Likewise, lines 3 and 4. The rhyming pattern should not be the same in the following stanzas. It may flow as AABB, CCDD, and the like. It ends with a rhyming couplet, just like one in a sonnet regarding the subject. Source: Spence, Sr., Joseph S. "Spirit of Nature: APO Anthology of Poetry." *APO Anthology of Poetry.* 2019.. https://anthologyfive.blogspot.com/2019/04/joseph-s-spence-sr.html.

Tanka poem: A fifth-century Japanese poetic form, it has a total of thirty-one syllables written in five lines of five, seven, five, seven, seven syllables. One may say that the senryu and the haiku, which were derived at a later date, are shorter versions of the tanka. Source: Turco, Lewis. "Lyrical Poetry: Tanka Poem." *The Book of Forms: A Handbook of Poetics, Vol. 3.,* 273. New Hampshire: University Press of New England 2000.

Tercet poem: Consists of three lines. Source: Padgett, Ron, ed. "Tercet." In *The Teachers & Writers Handbook of Poetic Forms,* 189. New York: T & W Books 2000.

Terza Rima poem: A form with an eleven-syllable count in each line and a rhyming scheme of aba, bcb, cdc, dd. Source: Turco, Lewis. "Lyric Poetry: Terza Rima." In *The Book of Forms: A Handbook of Poetics, Vol. 3.,* 275. New Hampshire: University Press of New England 2000.

Tosca 42 poem: A form created by Patricia Ann Farnsworth-Simpson; January 10, 2011. It starts by taking a three-letter word to use as an acrostic. The first line rhyme with the third line, both of these lines have a six-syllable count. The second and middle lines are written with an eight-syllable count that is split into four to make a double rhyme scheme within one line, thus making the poem's rhyming scheme. There is a minimum of three stanzas. Source: Farnsworth-Simpson, Patricia A. "Tosca 42 Poem." *Worldwide Alliance of Poets.* 2011. http:// pfppublishers.com.

Triolet poem: A poetic form consisting of only eight lines. The first, fourth, and seventh lines repeat. The second and eighth lines repeat as well. The rhyme scheme is simple: ABaAabAB. The capital letters represent the repeated lines. Source: Turco, Lewis. "Lyric Poetry:

Triolet." In *The Book of Forms: A Handbook of Poetics, Vol. 3.,* 277–78. New Hampshire: University Press of New England 2000.

Triple Strata poem: Created by Jan Henson, it has three lines. The first line has four syllables. The second and third lines have six syllables. The rhyme sequence is Aab, ccb, ddb, eeb, and so on. It may be about any subject and have any number of stanzas. Source: Henson, Jan. "Triple Strata Poem." *Worldwide Alliance of Poets*n.d. http://pfppublishers.com.

Triquatrain poem: A form of quatrain poem in tri-rhyme format, it has a specific rhyming pattern. Lines 1 and 3 have internal rhyme, while lines 2 and 4 do not. Source: "Triquatrain Poem." *Worldwide Alliance of Poets*n.d. http://pfppublishers.com.

Trolaan poem: Created by Valerie Peterson Brown, this poem consists of four-quatrain stanzas. Each stanza's line begins with the same letter. The rhyme scheme is abab. The content and syllable count are optional. Source: Brown, Valerie P. "Trolaan Poem." *Worldwide Alliance of Poets*n.d. http://pfppublishers.com.

About the Author

Joseph S. Spence Sr. is a professional poet, author, speaker, man of God, researcher, and book reviewer. He is the author of four collections of poetry and coauthor of six poetry collections. He served as a United States Army commissioned officer of twenty-six years honorable service, and also as a lay minister with designated military Chaplains. He holds several degrees, including one in divinity from Faith Theological Seminary. He is currently a member of Siloah Evangelical Lutheran Church in Milwaukee, Wisconsin.

Additional Books by Joseph S. Spence Sr.

➤ Trilogy Moments for The Mind, Body, and Soul (Amazon 2006)

> The Awakened One Poetics (Amazon Kindle 2010)

> A Trilogy of Poetry, Prose, and Thoughts: For the Mind, Body, and Soul (Amazon Kindle 2019)

He resides in Milwaukee, Wisconsin. His Website is https://www://trilogypoetry.com. His email is trilogypoetry@yahoo.com. His Facebook page is https://www.facebook.com/profile.php?id=100035897858755, and his LinkedIn page is https://www.linkedin.com/in/joseph-s-spence-sr-3a8a0a186/.

Review Request

Dear inspired reader, thank you very much for spending the time to read the uplifting words in "Sincerely Speaking Spiritually." We will be grateful if you leave a short review on Amazon.com and GoodReads.com to let us know what you think of our book as soon as possible. I am always impressed and encouraged to read the great words from readers. I listen to what they have to say, and it inspires me to write more. Thank you very much, and have a great day!

Several years ago, when **Sincerely Speaking Spiritually** was first published, I was asked, "What was your motivation for this book to make it such a dynamic and successful spiritual poetic text?" Some of my assertions follow.

This innate motivating body of knowledge constitutes the framework for **Sincerely Speaking Spiritually.** It demonstrates a faith-based foundational background as the springboard that sparks the flames traversing worldwide humanity while observing and proliferating inspirational knowledge of God's infinite light and graciousness into the common era. Humanity agrees this is a dynamic enlightenment to obtain and realize from God's grace!

Accordingly, meditational reflection is not a discourse on a subject that is generated overnight. This journey has taken valuable time. Naturally, space and time are vital, coupled with the historical dedication not to surrender to negativity. Alternatively, surviving the fight against the devil's effort of trying to drag one's mind, body, and soul down into the deep and dark abyss dungeons of hades where God is seen as disgusting, disgraceful, diabolical, and non-dialectical, and where the devil's demised demons are burning in hell's fire; thus reflect the enduring power of God's dynamic saving grace, which still is the great mantra for humanity. God's words state, "Let not your heart be troubled, neither let it be afraid." These are still great, uplifting, and dynamic words of God's grace to humanity. His words also state, "In keeping with God's promise, we are looking forward to a new heaven and a new earth, our home of righteousness" (2 Peter 3:13).

The following certificates, accolades, and course completions, which inspired its publication, highlight the inspirational path to this common era.

First is my baptismal and confirmation certificate from Arch Deacon Maxwell at St. Luke. It established a path to knowing, acknowledging, and living with God's Holy Spirit, nature, edifying instructions, and receiving His nurturing The Bible states, "Let us then approach God's throne of grace with confidence, so that we may receive His mercy and find grace to help us in our time of need" (Hebrew 4:16).

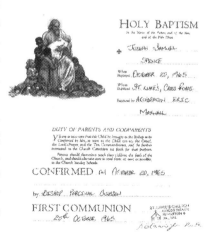

117

While working as a delivery driver for a Jewish Dry Cleaner in New York City, I had the opportunity to observe, understand, and participate in Jewish ceremonies and events at their businesses and residences. I had to make deliveries and collect decorative window drapes for cleaning and rehanging them. That was a great learning experience of the Jewish faith and practices.

Subsequently, while serving with the United States Army Worldwide Rapid Deployment Force in Ft. Liberty, North Carolina, I was asked to be a Eucharist Minister for the soldiers and their family members. In September 1981, I accepted and completed a course of studies with the Episcopal Bishop of the Armed Forces, Reverend Charles Burgreen. The teachings were upliftment from the body of Christ, God's goodness, and the church's centrality.

OFFICE OF THE BISHOP FOR THE ARMED FORCES
THE EPISCOPAL CHURCH

BE IT KNOWN BY ALL MEN THAT

J O S E P H S. S P E N C E

has satisfactorily completed

The Study Course for Members of the Armed Forces

This Course of Study is based on The Church's Teaching Series.
It involves assigned lessons and discussion.

25 SEPTEMBER 1981
Dated

Bishop for the Armed Forces

THE EPISCOPAL CHURCH CENTER — 815 Second Avenue — New York, New York, 10017

LICENSE FOR LAY MINISTRY

ISSUED BY THE BISHOP   FOR THE ARMED FORCES

For Service in the Military Establishment
of the United States

This is to certify that   *Joseph S. Spence*

upon the recommendation of CHAPLAIN EUGENE X. ZEILFELDER   is hereby authorized
to serve as   LAY READER & CHALICE BEARER   under the direction of
CHAPLAIN EUGENE X. ZEILFELDER   for a period of one year from this date

In fulfilling this ministry the directions of the Supervising Chaplain and the Constitution and Canons of the Episcopal Church will be obeyed

Signed at the Episcopal Church Center in the City
of New York, this 11th day of   November
in the year of our Lord 19 81   and in the
FOURTH   year of our Consecration

Suffragan Bishop for the Armed Forces

Thereafter, I assisted protestant chaplains in the United States Army during my worldwide assignments. Two certifications follow for Chaplain Zeilfelder, Ft. Liberty, North Carolina, November 1981, and Chaplain Maddox III, West

Germany, February 1985 These were dynamic and practical applications of God's words to His people. Accordingly, God's great commission states, "Go therefore and make disciples of all nations, baptizing them in the name of the Father and the Son and of the Holy Spirit" (Matthew 28:19-20).

Years later, upon reassignment to Ft. Riley, Kansas, USA, from Westen, Germany, I worshipped with Pilgrim Baptist Church, where some of my military friends attended. They asked me to speak to the church one day. Thereafter, they convinced me to stay and requested that I prepare and deliver a sermon. After that, I was certified as a licensed Baptist minister of the Gospel in July 1986 by Pilgrim Baptist Church. Their acceptance and affiliation took me on a dedicated spiritual journey across Kansas, articulating God's saving message to many.

Some months later, I became a member of the Christian Legal Society to enhance my knowledge of church operations and church and state issues in June 1987. During this process, I learned about technical issues confronting the Church and how to address them.

Christian Legal Society

hereby certifies that

Rev. Joseph S. Spence, Sr.

is a member in good standing of Christian Legal Society and fully subscribes to its principles and ideals.

June 14, 1987

President

Secretary

While assigned to Ft. Riley, Kansas, I completed a bachelor's in divinity from Faith Theological Seminary in March 1988. This improved my Biblical knowledge and opened a fountain of flowing water, quenching the thirst of congregations

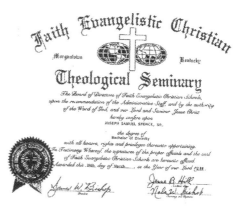

for God's gracious words. It also enhanced my knowledge of the Scripture, which states, "Study to show thyself approved unto God" (2 Timothy 2:15).

Simultaneously, I assisted the Diocese of Kansas, St. Paul's Episcopal Church, Manhattan, Kansas, while worshipping at Pilgrim's Baptist Church, and received a certification as a Lay Eucharist Minister in May 1988 from Bishop Grein. The differences between one congregation being predominately white and the other African Americans allowed God's words to permeate the souls of both. There are no color barriers to God's graciousness and salvation. Naturally, God says, "Whosoever will let Him come" (Mark 8:34).

I completed the Clergy, Tax, and Law course in February 1990. It was very beneficial and gave me advantages in providing consultation and assistance to pastors and their churches regarding such

Clergy, Tax and Law

THIS IS TO ACCREDIT

JOSEPH S. SPENCE, SR.

SEVEN CPE CREDITS
IN RECOGNITION OF SUCCESSFULLY COMPLETING
THE CLERGY, TAX AND LAW SEMINAR
AND THE ENCOURAGEMENT OF INDIVIDUAL
GROWTH, AND TO PROMOTE EXCELLENCE
IN MINISTRY FINANCES.

IN WITNESS WHEREOF THIS CERTIFICATE IS ISSUED

Certificate Number 4513

Date Feb. 15, 1990

Clergy, Tax and Law

CHAIRMAN

EXECUTIVE SECRETARY

requirements. The Bible says, "Do whatever it takes to be thoroughly grounded in the truth" (Ephesians 2:19-20).

I eventually relocated to Milwaukee, Wisconsin, as an assistant professor of military science for Marquette University Army ROTC program and joined Jerusalem Missionary Baptist Church as an associate pastor. I served with Reverend Donnie Sims, Pastor and President of the Wisconsin General Baptist Convention. While there, he convened an ordination board, which I completed with due diligence. He was ordained by Jerusalem Missionary Baptist Church and Wisconsin General Baptist Convention in August 1990 as a Baptist Minister.

In reflection, Moses ordained Joshua when God said unto him, "Take thee Joshua the son of Nun, a man in whom is the spirit and lay thine hands upon him; set him before Eleazar, the priest, and before the congregation; and give him a charge in his sight" (Numbers 27: 18-21). Accordingly, I was given a charge in God's sight.

While in Milwaukee, I became an Alpha Phi Alpha Fraternity member and served as the fraternity chaplain. This involved more than just delivering opening and closing prayers at the fraternity meetings. I was also involved in article writing and prayers at public events. I also worked with university fraternity members from the first to the highest degree of academic studies. The Bible states, "The Lord wants to use you for special purposes, so clean yourself from all evil. Then you will be holy, and the master can use you" (2 Timothy 2:21-26).

Many years later, I attended St. Mark African Methodist Episcopal (AME) Church in Milwaukee, Wisconsin. Many of my Alpha Phi Alpha Fraternity brothers worshipped there, including many friends I knew from the community. I served in various capacities while there to help build God's kingdom. While there, I studied the foundational creation of the AME Church and acquired significant knowledge. The Bible states, "Study to show thyself approved unto God" (II Timothy 2:15).

During my travels, Patricia Ann Simpson asked me to be a co-founder and poetry chaplain for the Worldwide Poetry Alliance, founded in Kent, United Kingdom. This position opened a floodgate of prayer requests from members and their families. I remained in that position for seven years. Every week, I received and completed many prayer requests.

The English version of this inspirational and uplifting poetry volume, **Sincerely Speaking Spiritually**, was published thereafter by WestBow Press, with the latest revised edition in 2020.

Along the path of spirituality, I came across various Christian organizations and became affiliated with them to strengthen my position and enhance my journey. One is Universal Ministries in Illinois, where I obtained a non-denominational ordination in November 2005. The Bible states, "I will lift my eyes unto the hills from when comes my help. My help cometh from the Lord, Maker of heaven and earth" (Psalm 121).

The American Association of Christian Counselors sponsors many seminars and certification courses to keep one abreast with the dynamics of God's kingdom in which I participated. God's words state that one should join with the saints for strength. Accordingly, "The prayers of the saints rise before God, and then God acts on earth" (Revelation 8:3).

Universal Ministries also presented a Doctorate in Religious Theology (honoris causa) based on satisfying their requirements to uplift God's kingdom and His people in July 2020.

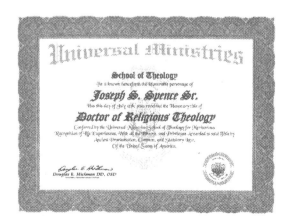

Madison-Jefferson Seminar regarding church and state issues provided excellent educational highlights, which allowed me to continue serving God's people. This seminar was on point with the Scripture, which states, "Keep this Book of the Law always on your lips; meditate on it day and night, so that you may be careful to do everything written in it. Then, you will be successful (Joshua 1:8).

My advocacy for God's grace and righteousness in uplifting humanity resulted in me receiving *The 2023 Rahim Karim World Literary Prize Award.* This is a manifestation of the Bible, which states, "Whosoever is kind to the poor lends to the Lord, and he will reward them for what they have done" (Proverbs 19-17).

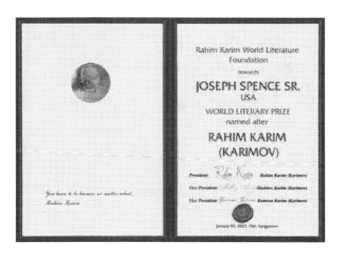

My inspired proliferation for peace, quality of mind, body, and soul, and the inspirational uplifting of God's kingdom for all people resulted in me receiving the **Mahatma "Bapu" Gandhi Global Prestigious Award** from India.

My quest for righteousness, an inspired quality of life, and God's grace in all people resulted in me receiving the **Indonesia Ambassador Award for Peace, Social Justice, Human Rights, and Diplomacy for the Indonesia Martial Arts Kingdom.** The Bible states, "May we shout for joy over your victory and lift up our banner in the name of our God" (Psalm 20:5).

My inspirational writings and advocacy for world peace and understanding resulted in my book, "The Awakened One Poetic," receiving the **Certificate of Honor for World Peace, Unified Faith, International Understanding, and Co-Existence** from Galaxy

126

International Foundation, India. This award manifests the word of God, which states, "The generous will themselves be blessed, for they share their food with the poor" (Proverbs 22:9).

My relentless pursuit of obtaining world peace, diplomacy, God's love in the hearts of humanity, and His graciousness permeating their minds, bodies, and souls resulted in me receiving the ***Attorney and South African President Nelson Mandela Prestigious Award for Peace and Equality in Literature.***

Based on the foregoing manifestations, it is obvious that recognition comes from all angles and directions when one is on the right path of uplifting God's graciousness, inspiration, equity, justice, righteousness, and quest for humanity's unending love in God's grace.

Thanks to the former Governor of Arkansas and 42nd United States President William Jefferson Clinton for the recognition as an *Arkansas Goodwill Ambassador* resulting from me helping first-generation students entering graduate school during a summer seminar at the University of Arkansas, Little Rock, Arkansas, and helping citizens of Little Rock, to established goals and milestones and reaching them with success from God's motivational uplifting grace. God states, "In all things I have shown you that by working hard in this way we must help the weak and remember the words of the Lord Jesus, how He Himself said, 'It is more blessed to give than to receive'" (Acts 20-35).

Grace and praises go to my Congressional Representative Gwen Moore for her *Congressional Recognition Commendation* with God's love for humanity exemplifying my work. God's words state, "And let us not grow weary of doing good, for in due season we will reap if we do not give up" (Galatians 6:9).

My dedication to serving God's people with graciousness and inspiration led me to receive the State of Wisconsin Certificate of Achievement from Wisconsin's Governor, Tony Evers, in November 2023 for winning the Zablocki Local Veteran's Creative Arts Writing Competition for four consecutive years from 2020 to 2023.

It is a beautiful realization that God works in mysterious ways based on His infinite powers. Regarding such, friends in Italy asked me to translate my book into Italian so they could read it. While contemplating the process and praying about it, I received a message from Knight Silvano, Italy, the founder of the **World Union of Poets-Italy,** a poetry association with several thousand members, who stated, "I am nominating you for a position in the organization." I greatly expressed my thanks. Ten days later, almost 200 people voted for me. This resulted in me being sworn in as the **President of the High Disciplinary Council, World Union of Poets-Italy.** I also have a deputy, a secretary, and two investigators. God states, "He shall be like a tree planted by rivers of waters, that brings forth its fruit in its season, whose leaves shall not wither, and whatever he does shall prosper (Psalm 1:3). This is being planted by rivers of water bringing forth fruits.

I am now a member of Shiloah Lutheran Church and School, a great congregation. My pastor, Reverend Bradley, wrote the forward for my tenth inspirational poetry book, Sincerely Speaking Spiritually. This book is being translated and published in Spanish. Members of the congregation love it.

Thank you very much, my dear brothers and sisters, for God's inspirational grace for reading this afterword, enlightening revelation of God's graciousness, and for my dedicated contribution to uplifting God's grace and building His kingdom. The journey in God's grace continues until the next edition coming soon.

Please have a wonderful day, and I pray that God's richest grace and blessings, surpassing all understanding, will rest and abide with you, your loved ones, your endeavors, and your family members always!

USA Goodwill Ambassador (appointed by USA 42nd President William Jefferson Clinton), Professor Dr. Joseph S. Spence Sr. (Epulaeryu Master)!

https://allauthor.com/images/reviews/gif/17520.gif

https://www.amazon.com/Joseph-S-Spence-Sr/e/B0855CYRPS?ref_=dbs_p_ebk_r00_abau_0

Printed in the United States
by Baker & Taylor Publisher Services